Table of Contents

Foreword

"Just experienced an earth quake in Tokyo on the way to the venue."

"We're currently sitting in traffic on a bridge. Pretty scary stuff."

"And now another one whilst on the bridge, perhaps that was an aftershock - scary".

"Finally got some phone signal back. Thank you all for your messages. We are all fine. Concert cancelled and we are on our way back to hotel."

At 2:26 pm Tokyo time (JST), March 11, 2011, members of the BBC Philharmonic Orchestra tweeted these messages as they were travelling from Tokyo to a concert in Yokahama, Japan. A 9.0 earthquake had slammed into the eastern seaboard of Japan, followed by a massive 23-foot tsunami just moments later.

Within seconds, the news had travelled the world, via Twitter, Facebook, YouTube, Skype and other social media networks. Governments leveraged Twitter for updates and media organizations like CNN and CBC communicated via Skype to communicate with their colleagues in Japan. U.S. citizens stranded in Japan posted updates to Facebook:

"over 8 million people stuck here in Tokyo as the trains, subways, etc are shut down. It's a site to see, I've never seen anything like it. Also the Airport is closed."

Matt Poll, serving in the U.S. Navy near Tokyo posted this to his Facebook page:

"Felt like i was back on my ship. Floor started rocking and i got vertigo."

Within a few days, the Japanese Prime Minister's office created an English-language Twitter account: @JPN_PMO - with this as the first tweet:

```
"Since the 8.9-magnitude earthquake hit Japan Saturday, social media has
played a vital role in reconnecting victims with loved ones and providing
real-time information about the crisis."
```

Instantly, we know and connect...via Social Media.

Social Media has become an integral and critical part of our lives in a very short period of time.

And yet, the topic elicits varying reactions ranging from fear ("it's all just a bunch of hype, it'll go away") to curiosity ("I've heard of it I think, should I be doing something about it?") to active participation ("Yes, I have a Facebook profile, and I'm changing how I market my business") to intense evangelism ("It's the best thing since cell phones!!!").

Why is Social Media having such an impact on us? What is it about Facebook that's so compelling? And why should businesses take it seriously?

The biggest reason by far is that Social Media tools like Facebook have shifted control from large media corporations to individuals. It's put the power to inform, publish, share, collaborate *and* engage squarely in the hands of ordinary people like you and me. Anyone who has news, an opinion, a thought, a review, or an idea can publish it directly online and in front of millions of people.

There is tremendous power to that. Understandably, it's a frightening concept for most businesses that have been used to doing things differently for a very long time.

Traditionally, businesses *tell* the consumer about products and services in arms-length transactions. With social media, we can directly *engage* with our customers and offer information of value that they can comment on, reply to, , recommend, review and share.
It requires a paradigm shift for businesses, not only to survive and succeed but to be competitive *and* excel.

The power to engage also brings risk – risk to being open, risk to our brand and even to our privacy. But that risk can be mitigated, by being prudent while being involved.

Be engaged, be where your *customers* are and take your business to another level – that's the power that Social Media offers. It raises the bar for all of us with new opportunities *and* new challenges.

If you're ready to meet that challenge, then this book is for you. Facebook is now a powerhouse in the world of Social Media, *surpassing Google as the number one visited site in the world in March 2010.* With more than 500 million active users and more than 50% logging on in any given day, more than eighty percent of the top 100 websites in the US have integrated with Facebook and more than 50% of the top global websites.

Facebook's phenomenal growth was the impetus for this book. Businesses are jumping onto Facebook in droves, because they've recognized its potential. As the prime destination for online users and *your* customers, this is the place you *must* be if you have a business.
My goal with this book was to provide a simple and easy-to-understand practical manual on how to get your business easily and effectively on Facebook, with as much visual help and as little technical jargon as possible.

I hope you find your journey through this book as engaging as it has been for me to write.

- Roohi.

Roohi Moolla, CEO/Founder
SocialBizNow | A Real-World Guide to Social Media
www.SocialBizNow.com

Connect with me on:
Twitter: @roohimoolla
Facebook: www.facebook.com/roohimoolla
LinkedIn: http://www.linkedin/in/roohimoolla

SocialBizNow is a resource and information blog portal on social and digital media, technology and the web. You can subscribe to the free weekly email SocialBizNow newsletter on http://www.SocialBizNow.com..

Introduction

Facebook in 14 Days!
A Practical Guide to Get Your Business Online

"If I have seen farther than others, it is because I was standing on the shoulders of giants."

- Sir Isaac Newton, English Mathematician and Physicist
(1642-1727)

Once intentionally the exclusive arena for college-students to hang out and socialize online, Facebook has fast become a giant in the world of business.

With hundreds of millions of people now on the most popular social platform in the world, the sheer numbers alone (500 million users and counting, and 23+ hours per month on average) are staggering - and reason enough for marketers and businesses to get excited.

The opportunities to connect with and discover more about customers in ways that were previously unimaginable through "Likes", "Friends", "Movies", "Music", "Info", wall posts, comments, conversations, photos, videos, and relationships, makes Facebook into a "personalized platform" that offers opportunities for the ultimate in a customized experience for the visitor.

For businesses, it's a whopping goldmine of eyeballs, potential markets, user data, customers and yes, absolutely, revenue. So, if you'll excuse the weird metaphor – how do you get your piece of that eyeball pie?

If you're like most businesses, you've already heard that you need a dedicated "business Page" on Facebook. Or perhaps you've already got a brand new Facebook Business Page?! Well, unless you get out there and *actively* promote your page, it's just like any other marketing tool in your toolbox - it's just going to sit there and gather dust unless you pro-actively tell people about it.

What You'll Learn

Whether you're a novice or already dabbling in Facebook, this book will show you, step-by-step, the fundamentals of how to set up a fully-functional, powerful Facebook business Page. With practical, easy-to-follow instructions, explanations, case studies, tips, examples, and numerous screenshots, you will be able to follow along with ease.

The Checklists and Worksheets attached to various Chapters are intended to help you get started on various activities referenced throughout the book. You'll also learn how to promote your Page and make it truly effective by posting great content, attracting visitors, building relationships, keeping them engaged - and converting them into customers.

What You'll Need

To complete the exercises in these chapters, you will need access to an Internet browser (e.g. Google Chrome, Safari or Internet Explorer). You will also need access to company logos and a few basic images in web-ready format (JPG, GIF or PNG files), plus some basic company information and initial content to start "seeding" your Page. So let's get started!

The Goal: A Great Business Page

The goal of this book is to help you understand Facebook business Pages and guide you through the steps of building a business Page that you can promote and help your business grow.

Before we begin, let's take a look at the anatomy of a business Page.

This is an example of a business Page that I designed for **Maid Brigade San Francisco East Bay & North Bay**, owned by Bruce Abbott.

It was built using the techniques that are described in the following Chapters. You will learn how to accomplish the major components of what you see on these pages, including the Profile Picture, the Custom "Get a Coupon" Tab, integrating Twitter and connecting your Facebook Page to your business Blog.

The goal for you will be to build a business Page with similar elements to this one, with your branding, logos, design and content.

Example of a Business Page
- The Wall

Profile Picture (max. size 180x540 pixels)

Top 5 Thumbnail Wall Banner

Admin Area - Admin thumbnails, frequently used menu links, promotion tools and Insights (Page metrics)

Edit Page button (only visible to Page Admins)

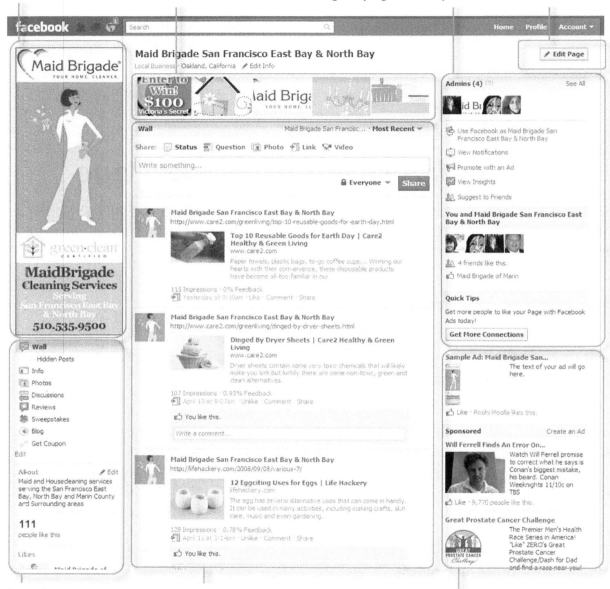

Main Tabs Menu, About box (text displays in searches), **# of Likes, Featured Pages, Featured Administrators**

The Wall - post Status updates box, filter Top News vs. Most Recent, post and comment Wall stream

Suggested Facebook Ad for current Page, **Sponsored Ads, Create an Ad** quick link

Example of a Business Page
- A Custom Welcome Tab

Page > Tab Name, Page Type, Geographic Location, Edit Info quick link

Admin Area - Admin thumbnails, frequently used menu links, promotion tools and Insights (Page

Personal Profile Menu - navigate Facebook as yourself, other Pages you administer and Help

Profile Picture (max. size 180x540 pixels)

Main Tabs Menu, About box (text displays in searches), **# of Likes, Featured Pages, Featured Administrators**

Application Tab - (max. width 520 pixels) - area that can be customized to display images, video, and "reveals" - different content for Fans vs. Non-Fans

Suggested Facebook Ad for current Page, **Sponsored Ads, Create an Ad** quick link

Day 1: Conduct an Audit

"The road of life twists and turns and no two directions are ever the same. Yet our lessons come from the journey, not the destination."

- Don Williams, Jr., American Novelist & Poet

Before you embark on your journey into Facebook, you need to know where you stand today. By conducting an audit of your current status, you'll have a good picture of your starting point and what you need to do to get where you need to go.

An audit is an essential place to start, and a task you should consider doing periodically across all your online properties, including your website, blog and social networks (Facebook Twitter, LinkedIn, YouTube etc.).

Depending on how active you are online, an audit is something you should consider doing every quarter, semi-annually or annually.

Step 1: Facebook General Audit

A General Audit will give a broad overview of the Accounts and Profiles you currently have on Facebook. If you already have a Facebook account or have multiple accounts, or someone else has set up an account for your business on your behalf, now is the time to record all those profiles and Pages. Whether you have a personal profile, a business Page, or even if you're not sure, the first thing you need to do is record some basic information about what you do have **before** you begin.

Use the Facebook General Audit Worksheet at the end of this Chapter to record what you currently have on Facebook, and give you a general overview of where you are today.

Facebook Profiles/Accounts

In the **General Audit Worksheet**, document all the current profiles and/or accounts you have set up on Facebook to-date. Include all personal profiles, business Pages, groups, and communities that your business is involved with - the more comprehensive your list, the better your analysis will be.

Unauthorized, Unused, Duplicate or Inactive Accounts

You need to know what has been created under your business name, authorized or not, including your company name as well as individually branded product lines.

If you have unused or inactive accounts, or are aware of unauthorized accounts created under your Business Name, make sure you include them in the list of accounts you're documenting. You may

decide to delete, re-activate or report accounts at a later date.

You also need to know if you have duplicate accounts which either you or your employees have set up.

For example, several employees at one company had set up multiple Facebook and Twitter accounts under various versions of the company name and were posting without consideration of the integrity of the company's brand or interests, let alone the potential liabilities that could arise.

Tip! Establish a Social Media Policy for your employees that covers your expectations for social media engagement. Include guidelines on: the kind of information that can and cannot be shared; frequency of posts; amount of time spent; separation of personal vs. business use; ethics; confidentiality; required approvals; and disclosure.

Poll your employees and ask them if any of them have set up Facebook accounts on your behalf, or using any of brand names for any of your products and/or services. Record the Account names and who set up the Account in the General Audit Worksheet. You can use this Worksheet later in the Managing Profiles & Pages section to help you decide which Accounts to keep, which to delete and which to deactivate.

Step 2: Facebook Detailed Audit

Facebook has a tool built into its business Pages called **Insights** that gives you some basic information about the activity on your business Page. If you already have a business Page, login to your account and click on the "**Edit Page**" button, then click on "**Insights**" on the left menu.

Record the information in **Insights** in the Detailed Audit Worksheet as a benchmark for the current activity on your Page.

 <u>Use the Facebook Detailed Audit Worksheet at the end of this Chapter</u> to record a current snapshot of results for your business Page. This will give you a starting place to measure against later.

Snapshot Example of Insights:

Include as much as you can about your visitors, pageviews, the number of comments, user experience, content and branding in the Worksheet.

This will give you an opportunity to measure what you accomplish as you progress, and provide some benchmarks on what you still need to work on at a later date. If you're not sure what to fill in on the worksheet, leave the spaces blank for now and complete the audit as you work through this eBook.

A detailed Audit of *each* profile or Page you have will help you determine which accounts are worth keeping, and which you may need to convert, deactivate or delete.

Content and Engagement

If you've started posting content on Facebook, document the frequency of your posting, as well as the type of content you post (e.g. personal vs. professional, once a week, twice a month).

Tip! Who and what other Facebook business Pages or people are you engaging with today? Do you know if any of your employees and customers talking about your company online? Use a tool like Google Alerts to set up keyword searches for the name of your company or competitors, and receive updates via email on when those words are searched, and the results they yield.

Integration

Integration refers to the linking of different social profiles. For example, your tweets (the status updates that you post on Twitter) can automatically appear on your Facebook profile, if you have enabled Facebook to allow this to happen. Document any and all

automatic relationships and integration you already have set up between Facebook and other websites, including posting from your blog to other article directories, search engines and channels.

One of the most challenging notions around social media is the amount of content that has to be posted on a consistent basis. If you're asking "Where am I going to find the time", there are several tools you can leverage to manage the time you spend on managing and posting content. We'll get into content posting tools in detail in a later chapter.

Integrating accounts allows content posted on one site to be posted to another automatically and can significantly reduce the amount of effort that's involved in posting to multiple profiles. Integration is enabled my many different social networking channels today.

Tip! Use the Facebook Detailed Audit Worksheet for *each* business Page or Personal Profile. Don't try and combine profiles into a single worksheet. If you don't have any Facebook accounts, just complete the basic information (Name and Date) in the Worksheet for your own information, and do an Audit later.

Take a current snapshot of results for your business Page, so you have a starting place to measure against later. Measurement give you statistics, the number of followers, friends and likes you have, the number of connections you have and so on.

Metrics are critical in your ongoing analysis, and an accurate snapshot of where you are today will serve to provide a great jumping off point when you need to compare what you've achieved later down the line.

SOCIALBIZ*Now*
A Real-World Guide to Social Media

Logos, Design and Branding

What does your brand convey today? Does your logo, brand, and tagline appear on your Facebook page?

Document any differences if you're using different graphics, logos, fonts, and styles across channels, including your website and blog.

Make sure that if you have specific product lines or brands, that you know whether any other accounts have already been created on Facebook with your product brand names.

Case Study: Coca-Cola

The story of Coca-cola on Facebook is classic (excuse the pun) - because it wasn't started by Coke. While the giant brand was sleeping at the wheel, two young guys, Dusty Sorg and Michael Jedrzeljewski, were searching for The Coca-Cola Fan Page on Facebook, and couldn't find one - so they created their own.

The page quickly became very, very popular. When Facebook implemented a new policy in 2008 that required pages promoting a brand to be operated by someone authorized by the brand, Facebook gave Coke

an option: we will shut down the page entirely, or we can hand ownership of the page over to you (Coke).

Coke was well within its rights to just take the page, along with all the fans, and leave the creators in

the dust. Instead, they chose to go to Facebook with a different option: let Dusty and Michael, the creators, continue to run the Coca-cola fan Page with help from a few members of Coca-Cola's interactive team. Coca-cola called Dusty and Michael, flew them to New York and the rest, as they say, is "history".

The lesson?

Monitor your brand, even if you think no-one's watching.

Example:

If you're a beer-making company named "California Beer Company", and you have 2 beers that you manufacture with the brand names of "Best Ale" and "Best Lager", make sure you look for all 3 names on Facebook.

How to Search for your Business or Brand

Login to your personal profile on Facebook. In the Search bar at the top of the page, start to type the name of the business or brand you want to search for. Results will appear as you type.

This is a screenshot for a search for **SocialBizNow**, which is listed in the **"Product/Service"** category for Organizations on Facebook.

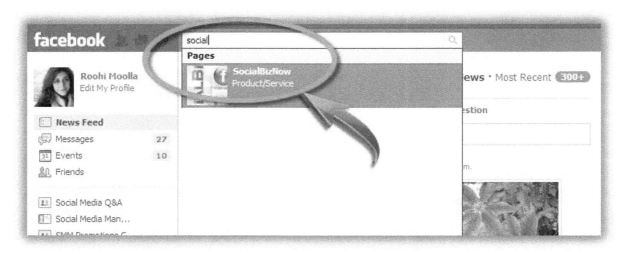

You may find multiple accounts with similar names, so make a note of each name and type of account (listed directly below the name) that you find that are related to your business.

You can see that in this next search, Coca-Cola has multiple Pages and is listed in multiple categories including "**Food/Beverages**", "**Public Figure**", and "**Company**", for different brands and product lines.

This search also returns separate pages for different languages, and different countries: **Coca-Cola New Zealand** and **Coca-Cola Australia**.

By the way, at the time of writing this book, the main Coca-Cola Page had
25,114,294 "Likes".

Facebook General Audit				
Business Name:				
Audit Date:				
Prepared By:				
Facebook Profiles and Pages				
Profile/Page Name (list all accounts including personal, business, brands, products & services)	**Active***	**Inactive****	**Account Type** (Personal, Business, Group, Community)	**Account Author**
Example.: Company ABC	x		*Business*	*John Smith*
Example: The Company ABC		x	*Personal*	*Lynn Jones*

* An account is Active if it has any one of the following:
- More than 1 Like or Friend
- Posts, comments, photos or other content posted to Wall
- Username has been registered

** An account is Inactive if:
- It has been deactivated
- There are no "Likes" or "friends"
- No posts, comments, photos or other content
- No username has been registered for the account

Facebook Detailed Audit

Audit Date:	
Prepared By:	
Profile Name:	
Page Administrators: (list names)	

Profile Details

	#	Notes
Branding/Content		
Wall Posts		
Branding		
Profile Picture		
Photos		
Videos		
Engagement		
Likes		
Visitors		
Comments		
Upgrades		
Custom Tab		
Welcome Page		
Other (Contest, Sweepstakes, Surveys, Polls...)		

Day 2: Set Goals

"Discipline is the bridge between goals and accomplishment."

- Jim Rohn, American Entrepreneur (1930-2009)

We all know that for business, the fundamental goal is to get customers and increase revenue, but how does that relate to Social Media, and in this case, Facebook?

Many people I speak with who are beginning to get their feet wet with Social Media say that they opened their Twitter, Facebook and LinkedIn accounts - even started "tweeting" and "posting" - but "just aren't really seeing much in the way of results".

My question to them is usually this:

"What goal do you have in mind with your Facebook Strategy?"

Most of the time, people are so excited about the possibility of connecting with potential clients and reaching so many people on Facebook that they jump in, feet first – and forget that the basic aspects of marketing still need to be honored.

Before embarking on your journey into Facebook, it's still essential to define your goals first.

What do you hope to achieve with your efforts? Is it to gain an audience, get more visibility, build relationships, decrease the number of customer complaints, increase the number of new clients, increase the number of referrals? How about increase traffic to your website? Or reduce the cost of lead acquisition? What about increase the amount of revenue per customer or launch new product ideas?

There are a lot of options, but only you can determine what's important to you.

Use the Goals Worksheets at the end of this Chapter to consider and define your goals for your Facebook business Page, and what you want to achieve.

Think about the basics first. Define your goals – think about what you want to achieve, and then start with some small but strategic steps to get there. Set aside a few minutes each day to make sure your goals are still aligned with your business strategy and direction, and be consistent and be patient.

While your mission statement is the long-term vision for your company, business goals are not your mission statement. Goals can change, adapt and adjust to changing conditions - your goals

may need to be flexible as your business grows, changes and responds to outside internal or external influences and conditions.

Be SMART

When defining goals for your business, use the **SMART** method to ensure your goals are:

S = **Specific**
M = **Measurable**
A = **Achievable**
R = **Relevant**
T = **Timely**

Specific

Define very specific goals using action verbs like "organize, improve, increase, decrease".

An example of a specific goal is

"*Improve* customer service by *decreasing* the number of calls we receive regarding our upcoming events."

Make sure you can answer the following questions:

- **What are you going to do?** (e.g. increase revenue, reduce complaints, improve customer retention)
- **Why are you going to execute this goal?** (e.g. to reduce costs, to improve visibility, to enter new markets)
- **How are you going to achieve the goal?** (e.g. launching a new product, writing an article series, training employees)

Measurable

To determine whether an online campaign or strategy is successful, you need to measure the current state vs. the new state. Depending on what you measure, your measuring units will be different.

For example, if you're measuring an increase in customers, you may measure by percentage or actual numbers of customers.

You may look at the difference in statistics over varying lengths of time, or compare your own statistics to a competitors numbers.

Achievable

Goals that aren't realistic are essentially a formula for failure. A goal that is slightly higher than the norm for performance can still be achievable, and can even lead to good things for a business including innovation and learning.

By the same token, a goal that is set too low has little value, and can be a de-motivator as well as seemingly inflate actual performance.

Relevant

Goals should be relevant to the actual work to be done. Many businesses are doing a majority of work that's not directly relevant or aligned with their goals or vision for the future - and this has a direct impact on whether those goals can be achieved.

Example: A relevant goal for a business that offers dental services might be "Reach 20% of adults under the age of 60 in our target market within 2 years". However, if the vision for the business is to serve the dental needs of ALL seniors, then this goal doesn't make sense, because it excludes anyone over the age of 60.

Timely

Goals should have specific starting and end points, with a limited duration. This helps to focus a goal within a timeframe and provides the opportunity to create checkpoints along the way.

Goals that don't have specific schedules are usually doomed to meander and react to the everyday activities and crises that invariably happen in any organization.

Example: An example of a timely goal is "Achieve 10% fewer customer complaints within the next 6 months."

Qualitative Goals vs. Quantitative Goals

Goals can generally be categorized into two types:

1. **Qualitative** Goals
2. **Quantitative** Goals

Qualitative Goals

Qualitative are "purpose-based" Goals and are the goals that align with your business strategies, are larger and broader in scope, generally more conceptual and usually more difficult to measure.

Example: An example of a purpose-based goal is **"Increase Brand Awareness"**.

Use the Qualitative Goals Worksheet at the end of this Chapter to define goals for your Facebook business Page.

Quantitative Goals

Quantitative are "metrics-based" goals that also align with your business strategies, but are more specific, generally targeted numeric goals that can be easily measured.

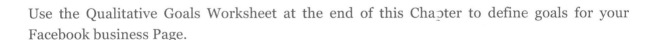

Example: An example of a metrics-based goal is **"Increase the number of visitors by 20% to our Facebook business Page over a period of 3 months."**

Use the Quantitative Goals Worksheet at the end of this Chapter to define goals for your Facebook business Page.

Qualitative Goals Worksheet

Business Name:	
Date:	
Prepared By:	

Description	Priority	Time Frame
Improve Visibility		
Attract qualified Job Applicants		
Improve Customer experience		
Establish Expertise		
Build relationships		
Launch Product		
Find and launch into new markets		
Research Competitors products/services		
Monitor and Manage online reputation		
Sell products/services		
Build a body of online knowledge		
Improve Brand Recognition		
Add your own goals...		

Quantitative Goals Worksheet

Business Name:	
Date:	
Prepared By:	

Description	Priority	Time Frame
Increase # of website pageviews		
Increase # of website unique visitors		
Improve SEO/Search ranking results		
Increase # of incoming hyperlinks		
Increase # of outgoing hyperlinks		
Build Email Subscribers List		
Convert visitors to qualified leads		
Increase # of paying Customers		
Increase Revenue		
Increase the number of online Conversations		
Increase quality content (videos, images, blog posts etc.)		
Increase the number of Comments posted		
Reduce the Bounce Rate		
Reduce the number of customer service intake calls		
Improve integration between social networks		
Reduce offline advertising budget		
Retain Existing Customers		
Improve the close rate (# of leads vs. # of customers)		
Decrease Cost to Acquire a Customer		
Increase Lifetime Value of a Customer		
Add your own goals...		

Day 3: Create a Business Page

"That some achieve great success, is proof to all that others can achieve it as well."

- Abraham Lincoln, US President (1809-1865)

Now that you've completed an Audit, you should have a clear picture of the Profiles and Accounts you already have on Facebook, if any. Now, you have some options. This chapter covers the complexities and differences between Facebook's different Profile and Account types. Once you understand the differences, and the pros and cons of each type, you'll be able to make a decision on which path you choose to create a business Page.

Managing Profiles & Pages

jug·gler noun \ j-g (-) l r\ -   "...one skilled in keeping several objects in motion in the air at the same time by alternately tossing and catching them.."
- Merriam-Webster Dictionary (m-w.com)

One of the biggest issues for businesses is managing all the accounts that suddenly seem to spring up when they first discover the world of Facebook.

You may have created some of those accounts yourself, or someone else might have done it for you. You may not even be aware of all the accounts that have already been created "on your behalf" by well-meaning employees, friends, acquaintances and sometimes even cyber-squatters.

So how do you manage all those accounts? Should you delete them? Consolidate them? Report them?

The answer is, it depends. There are lots of options, but you need to choose carefully depending on your particular situation. You can close, delete, convert or migrate, transition or just ignore your accounts - but each choice will have consequences.

A Comprehensive Primer on Profiles and Pages

Facebook has **six** types of profiles: three "profiles" for individuals and three "entity" types for organizations

and groups. Following is a detailed explanation of each type:

Individual Roles on Facebook

There are three types of individual roles on Facebook:

1. Personal Profile - A personal profile is an account that represents an individual who wants a Facebook profile for themselves to connect with their friends, family and community including other people, Pages, communities, and groups on Facebook.

A Personal Profile can be directly accessed with login credentials.

Keeping a Facebook profile for anything other than an individual person is a violation of Facebook's Statement of Rights and Responsibilities.

2. Business Account - A business account is an administrative account for an individual who *only* wants to administer **Official Pages** and their ad campaigns on Facebook.

A **business account** does not have the same functionality as a Personal Profile, it has limited access to information on the site, cannot be found in search and cannot send or receive friend requests.

An individual with a business account can view all the **Official Pages** and Facebook Ads that they have created, however they cannot view the profiles of other users on the site or other content on the site that does not "live" on the Pages they administer.

A business account can be directly accessed with login credentials.

3. Page or Group Administrator - A Page or Group Administrator is an administrative role for an individual who has been authorized to manage one or more Facebook **Official Pages** or **Groups**.

If you have been given the authority to be a Page Administrator, you are "automatically" in that role when you visit any business Pages you administer. There is no separate login from your personal profile.

Entity Roles on Facebook

There are three types of entity roles on Facebook:

1. Official Page - A type of account that represents entities like organizations, businesses, brands, celebrities, and bands to display and showcase information about themselves in an official, public manner to people who choose to connect with them.

Official Pages have some features that are similar to **Personal Profiles**, and can be enhanced with additional applications that help communicate, engage and capture audiences. Official Pages are intended to help an entity communicate publicly about themselves.

An **Official Page** can only be managed through the account of a **Page Administrator**, and can have 1 or more Page Administrators.

Facebook Official Pages provide more robust features for organizations, businesses, brands, and public figures including allowing multiple page administrators, having multiple custom page tabs and get post and page visitor statistics.

2. Groups - A membership based account for a group of individuals who want to communicate directly with each other and with the group about a specific subject. Groups can be created by anyone and about any topic, as a space for people to share their opinions and interest in that subject. Anyone can create and administer a group.

Groups are generally meant for smaller groups of people you know personally, and can be kept closed or secret. The features for groups are more collaborative, and are meant for easy sharing of content amongst the group members e.g. *Group Docs, Group Chat, Group Events.*

Groups are managed and maintained by one or more Group Administrators.

3. Community Pages display Wikipedia articles on various topics, as well as related posts from people on Facebook in real time. *At this time, Facebook does not have a way for you to add your own pictures or edit information on these pages.* Community Pages cover general topics, causes or experiences, and all kinds of unofficial but interesting things, sourced from Wikipedia.

Community pages may link from fields you filled out in your personal profile. You can "like" these pages to connect with them, but they aren't run by a single author, and they don't generate News Feed stories.

Click here for the Individual Roles vs. Entity Roles Chart - a Side-by-side Comparison Chart of the different Profiles and Accounts on Facebook.

Personal Profile vs. Business Page

Many businesses are still incorrectly using or setting up a "Personal Profile" on Facebook. Facebook personal profiles are supposed to be for and represent individuals, not businesses.

If you're a business, brand, organization or entity – not an individual – you should have a business Page on Facebook, NOT a personal profile. They are NOT the same thing.

The Difference between a Business Page and a Personal Profile

The biggest difference is that a business Page has "**Likes**" (what used to be called "Fans") while a personal Profile has "**Friends**".

In addition, personal Profiles don't have the same features as business Pages. For example, personal Profiles are limited to a maximum of 5,000 friends, whereas businesses can have unlimited likes.

SOCIALBIZNow
A Real-World Guide to Social Media

Facebook <u>Official Pages provide more robust features</u> for organizations, businesses, brands, and public figures, including multiple page administrators, multiple custom page tabs and post and page visitor statistics.

How do you know if you have set up a profile correctly or incorrectly for your business?

If you have "Friends" instead of "Likes", then you have a personal profile. A business Page should have "Likes" not "Friends" – and the visitor to your page would see the "Like" button at the top of the page, not the "Add As Friend" button.

Facebook Terms of Use

If have a personal Profile, and you don't convert your profile to a Page, you're at risk for permanently losing access to your profile as well as all of your content, including "Friends", photos, wall posts and comments.

Keeping a Facebook profile for anything other than an individual person is a violation of Facebook's <u>Statement of Rights and Responsibilities</u>.

Case Study: With humble apologies to the <u>Hyatt At Fisherman's Wharf</u>, this shows an incorrect use of a "**Friend**" page for an organization:

 Wrong:

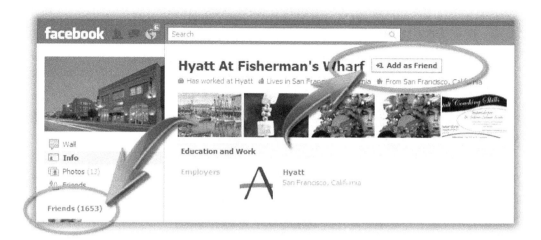

 Right:

Should You Convert Your Personal Profile to a Business Page?

Facebook has recently announced a new way to <u>convert your Facebook Personal Profile to a Business page</u>. This process is meant for only those individuals who have mistakenly setup a personal profile for their business, erroneously thinking they were setting up a business page. The process has some advantages, but also some very strict limitations.

One of the main advantages for converting your personal profile to a Business page is to convert all your friends into "Likes" of your business.

If you don't convert your profile to a Page, you're at risk for permanently losing access to your profile as well as all of your content, including "Friends", photos, wall posts and comments, let alone the time and effort you've spent on building those relationships.

 Important! **This is NOT for people who use their personal profile to communicate with friends, family, colleagues and associates** and who suddenly decide that all these people should now become fans of their business – you'll alienate a bunch of people if you do this.

If however, your "friends" are indeed business-related, and became "friends" with your "personal profile" which is actually a business, then now is the right time to make the conversion.

 Important! The account associated with the personal profile you previously maintained will be converted to a <u>business account</u>, which will be the sole Administrator of your new Page. **Do NOT do this conversion if you need to keep this personal Profile for any other reason.**

<u>Click here for the steps on How To Convert Your Facebook Personal Profile to a Business page</u>

Common Multiple Profile Problems and Recommendations

Let's look at the most common scenarios with business profiles setup incorrectly on Facebook, and look at the options, pros and cons for what you can or should do in each case.

Problem Description	Recommended Steps	Pros	Cons
Business set up as a Personal profile (Option 1)	1. Convert personal Profile to business Page	• One-step process • "Friends" automatically become "Likes"	• Personal Profile becomes business account with limited functionality • Lose all other content, including posts, photos, comments, videos etc.
Business set up as a Personal profile (Option 2)	1. Start new business Page and 2. Request "Friends" to become "Likes" on new business Page 3. Change Username on Personal Profile (if set) 4. Deactivate personal Profile	• Clean slate business Page • Opportunity to convert "Friends" to "Likes" • Personal Profile is hidden from searches • "Friends" may become "Likes" creating immediate fanbase	• Not all "Friends" will become "Likes" • "Personal Profile" still exists • Multi-step process
Business Page and a personal profile set up, both in your company name	1. Hide personal Profile and 2. Request "Friends" to become "Likes" on new business Page	• Personal Profile is hidden from searches	• Not all "Friends" will become "Likes" • Business "Personal Profile" still exists • Multi-step process
Multiple business Pages are setup, but you only use one, the others were "mistakes" or "trials".	1. Request "Friends" to become "Likes" on new business Page and 2. Delete unused business Pages 3. Report unauthorized pages to Facebook	• Single business Page will be the result, easier to manage and maintain	• Not all "Friends" will become "Likes" • If you are not the administrator of other Pages, you cannot delete them and will have to report them to Facebook • Time-consuming

Now that we've covered the differences between Facebook Profiles and Accounts, you should be able to make a decision on whether you need to start from scratch with a new business Page, or convert an existing Profile.

Create a Business Page

Step 1. Go to www.Facebook.com – **if you have an account, don't login yet!**

Step 2. Create a Page

If you don't have an account or are logged out, on the Facebook front page, click the link at the bottom that says "**Create a Page**".

Tip! There are alternate ways to find the Create a Page link, if you're already logged into Facebook. If you have a personal account already, Facebook buries the link to create a page in a few different places.

Click here to go to the Facebook start screen to Create a Business Page, or to find the link (buried in the Help Center), go to **Account > Help Center > Pages for Business >Creating and administering your Page > How can I create a Page?**

Step 3. Select a business type

You will now a screen with a number of different account option types. **Select the option that fits your business or organization.** The type of selection you make here will categorize your account and affect the type of interactions your users can have with you. For most businesses, you will either be a **Local Business or Place** (if you have a bricks and mortar business), or a **Company, Organization, or Institution**. Complete the fields that show up, which vary depending on business type you select., and click the "**Get Started**" button once you've completed the form.

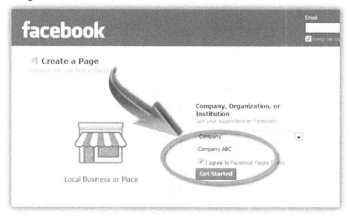

Facebook Pages come pre-installed with custom functionality for each Page category. These are the applications and information fields Facebook believes will be most relevant to the category you have selected when creating your Page. *For instance, a Band Page comes pre-installed with a music player, video player, discography, reviews, tour dates, and a discussion board.*

To control settings and add more applications, click "**Edit Page**" when you view your Page. You will see the applications that are currently available, as well as a link to add more at the bottom of the page "**Browse for more applications**".

Step 4. Complete the form
The next screen will ask you to complete a form.

If you DO already have a personal Facebook account, you can log in using that account, and you will then become an administrator of the new Business Page you're creating.

If you DON'T already have a Facebook account, fill out the form. Facebook will create an account for you that makes you an **Administrator** only of the new business page.

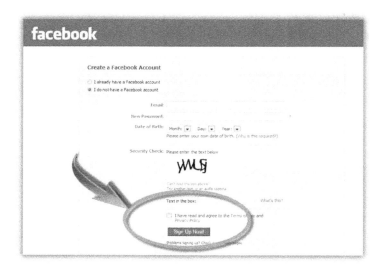

As an Administrator, you have **very limited permissions** to do anything else on Facebook other than administer the business page.

A Facebook business page Administrator Account is NOT the same as a Facebook personal Profile. Business Administrator accounts have very limited functionality on Facebook, including limited access.

An individual with a business account can view all the Pages and Social Ads that they have created, however they cannot view other users' profiles or other content on Facebook that does not "live" on the Pages they administer.

Complete the form and click the "**Sign up Now!**" button.

 Tip! "**Business accounts**" are for individuals and are NOT the same as a "**business Page**". They cannot be found in search and cannot send or receive friend requests. **If you have a personal profile on Facebook, use that one to administer your pages.** People will NOT be able to see your personal profile, personal photos or personal information on the business page, they are separate types of accounts.

If you already have a personal profile, you should not try and create a separate business account to manage business Pages because that would violate Facebook's terms regarding multiple accounts. Maintaining multiple accounts, regardless of the purpose, is a violation of Facebook's Terms of Use.

Fans of any Pages that you administer do not have visibility or access to your personal account or profile, and any actions that you take as a Page administrator on your business Page will show the Page's name, not your personal name.

 Tip! The most important thing to remember is that when you're posting to a Page and you want your business name to appear, you must be logged in to the Page as the Page administrator.

That's it!

You've now created a "blank canvas" for your business page.

It should look like this:

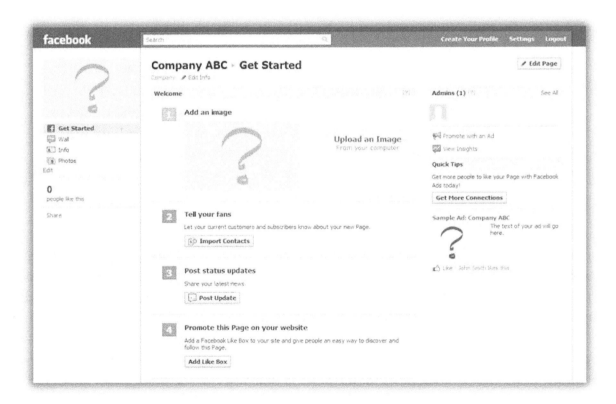

In the following Chapters, you'll learn how to add a Profile Picture, Tell Your Fans and Post updates to your Wall, and your Page will start to take shape.

If you've determined that you need to convert your personal profile to a business Page, follow these steps:

Convert Personal Profile to a Business Page

Before you begin, make sure you understand that when you convert a personal profile to a Page, **only**

- the profile pictures will be transferred,
- all that profile's friends will be automatically added as people who like the new Page.

Nothing else including any other content, including your wall posts, comments or other photo albums will be carried over to your new Page.

Tip! Make sure you save any important content before beginning your migration – download your Facebook content before you begin the process of converting your profile. Click here for a SocialBizNow blog post on How To Download Your Facebook Content.

Step 1. Login to your personal Profile on Facebook.

To begin the process of converting your Facebook personal profile to a business page, you *must* be logged in to Facebook.

Step 2. Begin Conversion

Type (or copy and paste) this address into your browser's address bar:

http://www.facebook.com/pages/create.php?migrate

Facebook will walk you through the steps of setting up a new Business page.

The account that you had as your personal profile will be converted to an _Administrator_ account of the new Business page.

How to Delete a Business Page

Note: In order to delete a business Page, you must be the Administrator of that Page.

Step 1. Login

Login to your personal Profile on Facebook.

Step 2. Access Page

Under "**Account**", click on "Use Facebook as Page".

A popup window with a list of the business Pages you administer will appear. Click the "Switch" button to switch to the Page you want to delete.

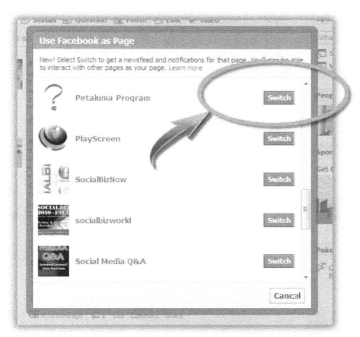

Step 3. Delete Page

Facebook in 14 Days! A Practical Guide to Get Your Business Online

- 59 -

Click the "Edit Page" button at the top right of the Page.

You will be on the Manage Permission screen as an Administrator. At the bottom of the screen, click on the "**Permanently delete *Page Name***" link.

If you're certain you want to delete the Page, in the popup window, click "**Delete**". You will see a brief confirmation message that the Page was deleted, and then be redirected back to the "**Pages You Admin**" screen.

Deactivating a Personal Profile

If you have set up a Personal Profile as a business Page, you can either <u>Convert Your Personal Profile to a Business Page</u>, or setup a new business Page and deactivate the Personal Profile that was incorrectly setup as the business Page.

 Tip! If you "deactivate" a personal Profile, the profile and all information associated with it disappears from Facebook immediately. People on Facebook will not be able to search for that Profile or view any of the information on that Profile.

If you want the personal Profile **permanently deleted with no option for recovery**, you can submit a request to Facebook to have the account removed. Log in to the Account you want to removed and then <u>click here to submit a request to Facebook to have your Profile permanently deleted.</u>

To delete a Personal Profile which has friends that you want to invite to your business Page, you need to complete all three of the following 3 steps:

1. **Invite your "Friends" to become fans of your new business Page**

To invite "**Friends**" to "**Like**" your business Page, send a Message to groups of up to 20 at a time (the maximum Facebook allows for each Message). Make sure you include a personal note with the request and include a link to your business Page in the body of the message to make it easy for your friends to find your business Page.

Steps to Send a Message to Friends

1. Login to your Personal Profile
2. In the left menu, click on "**Messages**", then click the "**New Message**" button on the upper right corner of the screen.
3. In the "**To**" box, start typing a name, and select the name of the person, repeat for each name.
4. Type your message and click "**Send**".

2. Change the username on the Personal Profile to an inactive name

If you already selected a username for the Personal Profile, you need to change the username so that people who find your account accidentally don't mistake it for your "real" business Page.

Steps to Change Username on Personal Profile

1. Login to your Personal Profile
2. From the "**Account**" menu on the upper right, click on "**Account Settings**".
3. Next to "**Username**", click on the "**change**" link
4. In the textbox, type in a name that is *unrelated* to your business name or brand e.g. "*temporaryPage1234*"
5. Click the "**Check Availability**" button, then confirm the name.

3. Deactivate the Personal Profile

To complete the process, you need to deactivate the Personal Profile you had set up as a business Page so it cannot be found in Facebook searches.

Steps to Change Username on Personal Profile

1. On the "**My Account**" screen, next to "**Deactivate Account**" click on the "**deactivate**" link.
2. Confirm to deactivate the account

Facebook Individual Roles vs. Entity Roles

	Personal Profile	Business Account	Page/ Group Admin	Page	Group	Community (Wikipedia-Sourced)
Has Profile Picture	✓	✓	✓	✓	✓	
Has Wall Posts	✓	✓	✓	✓	✓	
Has Comments	✓	✓	✓	✓	✓	
Can Have Photos/Albums	✓	✓	✓	✓	✓	
Can Have Videos	✓	✓	✓	✓	✓	
Has Top 5 Thumbnail Pictures	✓	✓	✓	✓		
Appears in Search Results	✓		✓	✓	✓	✓
Can be deactivated/deleted by self	✓	✓				
Has Friends	✓					
Has Likes ("Fans")			✓	✓		✓
Can register username	✓	✓	✓	✓		
Represents an individual person	✓	✓				✓
Represents organizations, businesses, bands, celebrities, non-profits, brands			✓	✓		✓
Represents a community or group					✓	✓
Has login credentials (can login directly to account)	✓	✓				
Is an Administrator Profile only			✓			
Managed by 1 or more Administrators			✓	✓	✓	
Requires Page Administrator rights to access account			✓	✓	✓	
Has Members (with approval)					✓	
Can be deleted by Page or Profile Admin	✓	✓		✓	✓	

Day 4: Page Settings and Administration

"An autobiography is not about pictures; it's about the stories; it's about honesty and as much truth as you can tell without coming too close to other people's privacy."

— *Boris Becker, World & Olympic Tennis Champion*

(1967-)

Facebook is a great online marketing tool - easy to use, relatively inexpensive, accessible at home, work or even on your mobile phone, and it levels the playing field for those of us who want a voice in the digital world.

As with any social media marketing tool, Facebook must be well managed and administered to be effective at reaching and engaging customers.

Beginning with privacy and security, this chapter deals with doing some of the initial "housework" necessary to administer your Page and covers an overview of the administration dashboard .

Privacy and Security

Privacy and security are issues that must be addressed and pro-actively managed on Facebook.

Whether you are a sole proprietor or you have multiple employees who are talking about your business, or working with sensitive data, or are engaged in promoting your product through various social channels, you need to make sure that you've created a very clear policy that addresses issues surrounding privacy and security of your information *and* your clients' information.

Create a clear work policy with expectations and guidelines on how you're going to address these important security issues:

1. **Privacy** – have a policy on what can and cannot be shared by your employees (client names, financial information, issues, personnel/HR information etc.), and a plan for what to do if you suffer the loss of sensitive data

2. **Viruses** – with Facebook leading the way, social networks are notorious for spreading viruses because people are so ready and willing to download shareware and freeware, especially applications their "friends" are recommending or sharing. Specify in your policy what is ok to download – and what is not.

3. **Reputation** – it's far easier to damage a reputation than to build a reputation. You work extremely hard to create your brand and business reputation so make sure that your employees and the voices that represent that brand are well aware of how you want your business to be represented, or if they need to have a disclaimer on their content that makes it clear when their opinion doesn't represent yours.

SOCIALBIZ*Now*
A Real-World Guide to Social Media

4. **Productivity** – Social networking can sometimes feel like a rabbit warren – easy to get lost just wandering around. How much time is too much time on social networks? If it's on behalf of your business and part of their job, maybe more time is ok, but if it's for personal use or is getting in the way of doing other work, then you need to specify how much time is acceptable to be spending on all these social channels.

5. **Performance** – with a significant increase in internet usage, downloads, uploads and possibility of downtime due to virus infections on social networks, company network performance can be very seriously affected. Make sure you have capacity and clarity around your network's performance and data security.

Issues surrounding Facebook's privacy policies are hotly debated these days. It's to be expected that privacy would be a contentious issue in an environment like Facebook where sharing and commenting is integral to the experience.

The approach I recommend is one of cautious enthusiasm - learn the tools, learn how to control them and use them to engage while making the utmost effort to respect people's privacy and comply with legal requirements.

Facebook takes its reputation on safety and privacy very seriously. It adheres to its' core principles by implementing a number of automated and other security systems, continuously reviews user profiles and accounts and shuts down accounts that don't comply with its' terms and policies.

However, it's your responsibility to manage your Profiles and Pages' privacy with the tools that Facebook provides.

If you have concerns, use the resources below for more information or contact Facebook directly for assistance.

Here's a list of resources for various aspects of Facebook's Privacy Policies, Guidelines and efforts:

Facebook Privacy Resources List

https://www.facebook.com/privacy/explanation.php

https://www.facebook.com/fbprivacy

https://www.facebook.com/safety

https://www.facebook.com/terms.php

https://www.facebook.com/communitystandards/

Facebook Page Privacy Settings

Facebook offers privacy controls for your business Page ranging from broad to granular that allow you to manage your business Page with flexibility.

Tip! As a Page Administrator, you can remove someone who has "**Liked**" your Page by clicking the "people like this" link above the "**Likes**" section of your Page, then clicking the "**X**" link next the user's name in the popup window that appears.

Page Administration Dashboard Overview

As a Page Administrator, you can control many aspects of your business Page. From Privacy and Permissions settings to Marketing your page and understanding the activity of your visitors, you can manage your business Page settings, from within your business Page administration dashboard.

To access the Page dashboard, login to Facebook and navigate to your business Page. Click on "**Edit Page**".

Manage Permissions

"**Manage Permissions**" is the default screen when you click "**Edit Page**".

Page Visibility: Check this box if you want to set your Page to "unpublished". It will not be available to public views or searches, and only Page Admins will be able to see the Page.

The "**Default Landing Tab**" allows you to select what view you want your visitors to see when they first arrive at your Facebook Page.

The default choice is the Wall, consisting of posts and comments. If you create a Custom Tab, the name of the Tab will appear in this list and you can opt to choose that Tab as your default landing Page for visitors.

This screen provides options for moderating lists of terms, and for choosing the appropriate security level for profanity, which filters the content that appears on your Wall based on Facebook's built-in library of commonly reported words and phrases that are considered offensive by the broader Facebook community.

You can also set the options for what your Page visitors can post to your business Page Wall in this section, whether they can write or post status updates, and post photos or videos.

 Tip! Once a visitor has "**Liked**" your Page, they will always go to the Wall when they land on your Page, no matter what you select for the Default Landing Tab.

Your Settings

Under the "**Your Settings**" link, review the settings that allow you to choose Posting Preferences and Email notifications.

As a Page Administrator, you automatically receive email notifications every time someone posts or comments on that Page. If you manage multiple Pages, you can manage your email settings from the Page Email Settings screen to choose email notifications for specific Pages.

To get to the Page Email Settings screen, click on the "**View all email settings for your pages**" link.

On the next screen, click the "**Change email settings for individual Pages**" link.

In the popup window, uncheck the box beside the Page for which you no longer want to receive emails. By default, all the Pages for which you are a Page Administrator are checked.

Basic Information

Click on the "**Basic Information**" link on the main menu of your Page dashboard to change settings for your business Category, and to complete other information about your business.

The more complete your information, the easier it will be for people to find you on Facebook and other search engines like Google. Fill out as much as you can here, including a link back to your website.

Your username is also visible on this screen. A username is the name you can choose that identifies your page address (or "vanity URL") on Facebook,

If you have more than 25 but less than 100 "**Likes**", you can edit your username on this screen.

All About Usernames ("Vanity URL")

A lot of people and businesses don't understand the importance of registering a username – or "vanity URL" as they are sometimes called – for themselves on Facebook.

Facebook usernames are like domain names – which is the address that people use to find your website on the internet. Similarly, a username is the address that people use to find you on Facebook – and you need to choose and register your username just as carefully as you did your website domain name.

Let's look at some Facebook username basics first.

What is a Username?

A username is part of your web address for your Facebook page.

e.g.www.facebook.com/yourusername

The default link that identifies your place on Facebook, whether it's a personal profile or business page is somewhat cryptic. It's usually pretty long, with a bunch of numbers:

e.g. *http://www.facebook.com/pages/mybusinessname/123456789*

But a lot "friendlier" link would be this:

http://www.facebook.com/mybusinessname

Much easier to type, and to remember!

Why else should you get a username? If you're a business, a friendly username helps your "branding", and is much easier to recognize and promote on other marketing material, online or offline.

A username is also known as a "vanity URL". When someone wants to visit your Page, they will be able to enter your username as part of the URL into their browser and go directly to your Page. (For those who've always wanted to know what URL means, it stands for **U**niform **R**esource **L**ocator.)

A Facebook username is also searchable. If someone enters your name as a search term on Facebook, Google or other search engines, the words you use for your username identify you and will be used to return results to the user if they're relevant. This is especially important if you're a business – if you register a username that isn't relevant to your brand, business or industry, you'll make it much harder for people to find you.

 Tip! While you need at least 25 "Likes" before you can register a username, a business username can't be changed after you have 100 "Likes".

Type in your name or business name into Google, and see what comes up for your Facebook address. Is it easy to read and understand? Are the words in the address relevant to your topic? If it's not relevant, it won't be easily found in searches.

As a domain name that' appears in search results as a hyperlink, a username is an important piece of Search Engine Optimization (**SEO**).

The words you choose in your username are keywords or phrases that someone may type in to a search engine, so choose your username carefully because it can affect your placement in search results.

Facebook has a lot of rules around usernames, so let's go over some of these in detail:

Facebook Username Rules

1. Personal profile usernames can only be changed once.
2. If you have a business Page, you can't register a username until you have at least 25 "Likes".
3. A Business Page username cannot be changed once it's created.
4. Changing your username also changes your Facebook email address (if you have one e.g.*youroldname@facebook.com* will now be *yournewname@facebook.com*) – and you will no longer receive email at the old address.
5. If your username is taken, you'll have to select another, as Facebook doesn't check to see if the username that you register matches your Page or profile name.
6. Your username must be at least 5 characters long.
7. Your username can only include letters and numbers (A-Z, 0-9), or a period or full-stop.
8. But wait! Just because you included a period, it doesn't make your username different from the same username without a period.

In other words, this

www.facebook.com/roohimoolla is the same as

www.facebook.com/roohi.moolla is the same as

www.facebook.com/ro.ohi.moolla which is the same as

www.facebook.com/r.o.o.h.i.m.o.o.l.l.a. – I think Facebook did this just to see if we're paying attention...

9. And, once you select a username, you can't change it – so choose carefully!
10. You can't register a regular word that's in everyday use as a username e.g. flower
11. Don't register a brand name that doesn't belong to you.
12. You can only have one username per Page or profile.
13. If someone has already registered a username that you wanted, you don't have a lot of options, so register your name now.

 Tip! **Don't cybersquat on a username** that might belong to someone else! It's against Facebook's rules. If you have a brand name, registered trademark or otherwise protected name that someone else has registered, you can appeal to Facebook to have it revoked.

There have been instances of Facebook removing entire pages like this one, including 47,000 fans, which had the word "realtor" (a word that's trademarked by the National Association of Realtors) in the username. It was eventually re-instated, but the username had to be changed.

If you are the owner (or authorized representative) of a brand or trademarked name, you can report an infringement on a username to Facebook with this form.

How to Get a Facebook Username ("Vanity URL")

Here are the steps to register your custom username/vanity URL on Facebook.

Step 1. Login to Facebook (yes, you have to be logged in)

Step 2. Go to the Username Registration Page

Type the username link **http://www.facebook.com/username** into the address bar of your browser, you'll see a page like this:

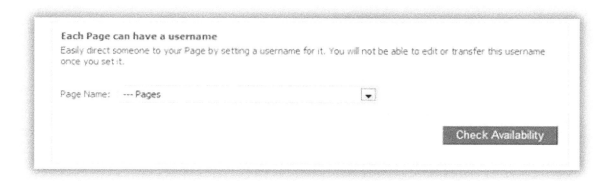

If you administer business Pages, you'll have the option to name those pages as well as your personal profile.

Step 3. Assign a Name
Select the page you want to assign a username to, and type in a username in the box that appears.

Click the "**Check Availability**" button to see if it's available.

If the name is available, you'll be able to confirm the username, if not – you'll have to select another name.

If this is a business Page you're setting a username for, and you get a message telling you the Page is "not eligible", it could be because you don't yet have 25 "likes".

Send a request (via Facebook Messages or Suggest to Friends feature) or an email to family and friends to "like" your page so you can reach your 25 minimum. This is Facebook's way of making sure that usernames are only reserved for Pages that are truly active.

If the username is already taken, you may see a message that says the username you selected is "not available". Try another name if this happens.

Remember to choose a username for your business carefully. Once it's created, you can't change it. Read the rules carefully before you click the "**Confirm**" button.

 Tip! You can register a username for your personal Profile too, just make sure you don't use something similar to your business Page username; the similarity will confuse your visitors when they search for your name, and they won't know which Profile to connect with.

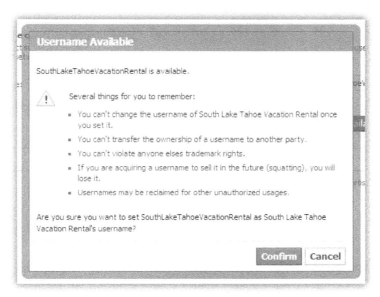

Click "**Confirm**" to finish reserving your username.

Once you've reserved your username, put it on your other marketing materials – including your business card, your website, your emails, brochures, advertising etc.

Tip! If you have a brick-and-mortar store, put your username in your store window, on your restaurant menu, on your receipts, customer surveys, wherever your customers might find you – it's great for business to help Facebook users to find you easily.

Profile Picture

The Profile Picture is a customized image or graphic that you can upload to represent your business on Facebook. It appears on the upper left corner of every screen of your Page, except Administration screens.

Click on "**Profile Picture**" in the administration Dashboard to edit your picture and for other editing capabilities.

You'll learn **How To Add a Profile Picture** in the next Chapter in detail.

The Featured Section

The "**Featured**" link allows you to "highlight" up to 5 other Pages and Page Owners on your own Page.

The Featured section appears on the left of your business Page, below your navigation menu.

To edit the "**Featured**" pages in this area, click on the "**Featured**" link in the Administration dashboard, then click the "**Edit Featured Likes**" button.

In the "**Edit Featured Likes**" popup window, check the boxes of the Pages you want to highlight on your Page, and click "**Save**". To view your changes, click the "**View Page**" button.

The "**Featured Likes**" Pages you see in the popup window is a list of your favorite Pages. To add more Pages to this list, click on the "**Add to My Page's Favorites**" link when you visit another Page.

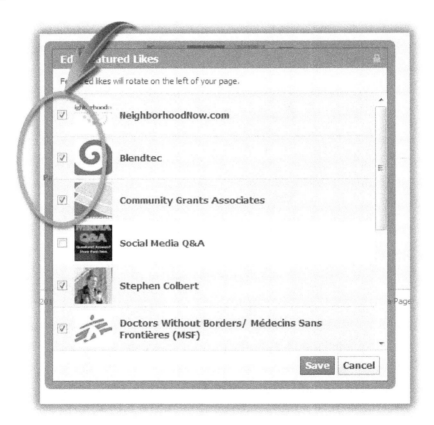

If you have multiple brands for which you maintain separate Pages, use the "**Featured Likes**" space to feature and cross-promote those brands.

Facebook in 14 Days! A Practical Guide to Get Your Business Online

- 83 -

Marketing

The "**Marketing**" screen has a number of different options to help you promote your page to get new visitors to your business Page, which we'll cover in detail later chapters.

 Tip! The "**Brand Permissions**" link at the bottom of this screen links to Facebook's own Branding Permissions and Guidelines page.

Manage Admins

Click on the "**Manage Admins**" link in the administration dashboard to add or edit Administrators for your business Page. Begin typing a name to see a list of possible names.

 Tip! If you are editing the Page using Facebook as a Page Administrator (not the Page itself), you can enter either a person's name OR an email address. If you switched to "Use Facebook as Page" (from below the Account link on the menu bar), you can only enter an email address in this box.

Using Facebook As Administrator

Using Facebook As Page

Applications

Facebook Applications (or "Apps") are "extensions" of Facebook's platform that allow the site to have more functionality and for visitors to engage and experience much more than just the primary Facebook platform itself. Some applications are built by Facebook developers, but most applications are built by outside developers.

A famous example of a 3rd-party application is Farmville, an extremely popular farming social network game developed by Zynga. Available on Facebook as well as an App for mobile phones, the game allows Facebook users to manage a virtual farm by plowing land, planting, growing and harvesting virtual crops, harvesting trees and bushes, and by raising livestock.

As of this writing, Farmville has **47,525,535** *monthly* active users.

Applications on Facebook allow increased interaction for Facebook users. You'll use applications in later chapters to enhance and increase engagement on your business Page. Click here to see examples of applications on Facebook.

Photos and Videos are examples of Facebook applications, and are installed as part of your business Page by default - as well as Links, Events and Notes.

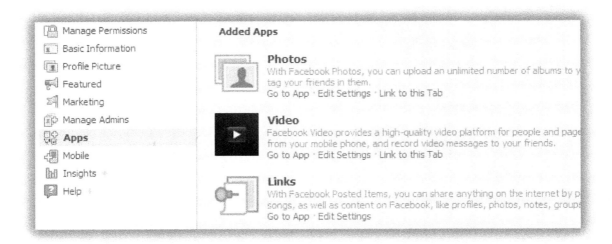

Mobile

Facebook is heavily integrated with mobile technology. You can use your cellphone to send Wall status updates directly Facebook by sending yourself updates which will automatically post to your Wall.

You can also receive status updates to your business Wall as text messages on your cell phone by clicking on the "Sign Up for SMS", and completing the steps to activate the service.

Insights

Facebook **Insights** is a free service that provides Facebook Page owners and Administrators with metrics around their content. Insights offers Page owners the opportunity to grow their business by understanding and analyzing trends on user growth and demographics, and engagement with content.

To see metrics on your Facebook business Page, click on **"Insights"** on the administration Dashboard. You will see a screen for the **Insights Dashboard**".

Only Page administrators can view Insights data for the business Pages they administer. To view comprehensive Insights on your specific business Page, click on the corresponding item on the left navigation bar.

If you are an Administrator of multiple pages, you can view the metrics for each Page by selecting each Page from the dropdown menu in the upper left corner of the dashboard.

Insights metrics is covered in detail in a later chapter.

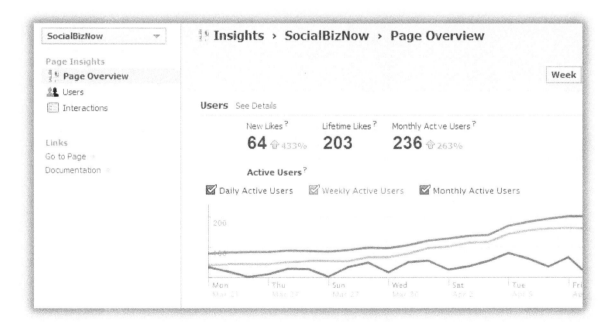

Day 5: Post a Profile Picture

*"Every man's work, whether it be literature or music or pictures or architecture or anything else, is always a **portrait** of himself"*

- Samuel Butler, British Author (1835-1902)

Now that you've setup your business Page on Facebook, you need to make it reflect your business. The first thing to do is upload an image that represents your business brand.

If you're a professional service provider, your logo plus some contact information is a minimum.

If you're a musician, artist or entertainer, you might choose to upload an image that reflects your work - or a particular piece. You can

also change your profile picture as often as you like, perhaps to highlight an upcoming event or product promotion. Use this space as an opportunity to showcase yourself, just remember this is your *business*. Don't put up a picture of yourself hanging out with your kids and expect people to realize this is a business page.

If you're a sole-proprietor with a service-based business, like a lawyer, accountant or real-estate agent- make sure you distinguish this page as a business page with more information than just your headshot. This is valuable real-estate on the screen, and you should use it to your best advantage.

A business profile picture should reflect the brand of the business plus have some basic contact information. Even better is a message briefly describing your services, a tagline and perhaps even a call to action. At a minimum, your profile picture should include
- your logo
- a tagline
- basic contact information

Think of your profile picture in a similar way to the header area on your website - it's the visual "anchor" for your Facebook Page(s).

Profile Picture Examples

Following are examples of good vs. not so good profile pictures:

Branded, strong identity, name and contact information!
https://www.facebook.com/lexus - Lexus
https://www.facebook.com/pages/Wonder-Bread-5/98596664755 - Wonder Bread 5
https://www.facebook.com/northbayhomesnow - Dana Kreuzberger, Realtor, Frank Howard Allen Realtors

Generic, no identification or contact information:
https://www.facebook.com/KGOMorningNews - KGO Morning News
https://www.facebook.com/pages/Hyatt-Vineyard-Creek-Hotel-and-Spa/194076054543?ref=ts Hyatt Vineyard Creek (Santa Rosa)
https://www.facebook.com/embassyofswedenwashingtondc - Embassy of Sweden in the US

A business profile picture should be appropriate , professional, with logo branding and with contact information.

Tip! The maximum size Facebook allows for a profile picture is 180 pixels wide x 540 pixels high. Pixels are the units that graphics software programs use to measure image size on computer screens. If you upload a picture larger than the recommended size, Facebook will resize the picture, and you will lose image resolution. Use a profile picture that is the same as the maximum recommended size, or smaller.

How-To Upload a Profile Picture

Step 1. Login

Before you begin, login to your business Page on Facebook, and go to the "**Get Started**" screen. You'll see this screen if you've set up an account, but haven't made any changes yet to your business Page. If you've already made some changes to your Page, click on "**Wall**" link in the left menu of the Page to see the profile Picture placeholder, which is an image of a big Question mark until you've uploaded a picture there.

Step 2. Upload a Profile Picture

Click on "**Upload an Image**" in the middle of the screen, or click on the "**Change Picture**" link – you'll only see this link if you hover over the big question mark on the left upper corner of your page.

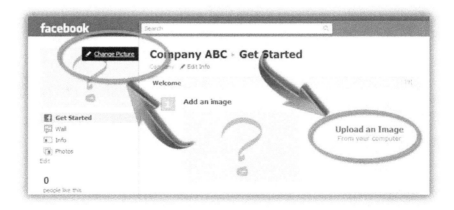

Step 3. Choose and Upload File

In the popup window, click on the "**Choose File**" button so you can find the image you want to upload on your computer.

This image should be a **maximum of 180 pixels wide x 540 pixels high,** the limit for Facebook's profile picture. **Browse** to the file you want, click **Upload** and then click **Okay,** all in the popup window.

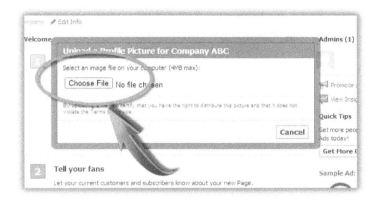

You should now see your picture appear on the left side of your Page.

You can change this picture as often as you like. To change the picture, hover over the profile picture again and click on the "**Change Your Picture**" link in the upper right corner. You can also go to "**Edit Page**" within your business Page and click on "**Profile Picture**" in the left menu.

Edit Thumbnail

The thumbnail is the image that shows up on all your Wall posts when you post to your business Page. It's a small snapshot Facebook takes of a portion of your Profile Picture.

Adjust the thumbnail by dragging it within the "**Edit Thumbnail**" popup window.

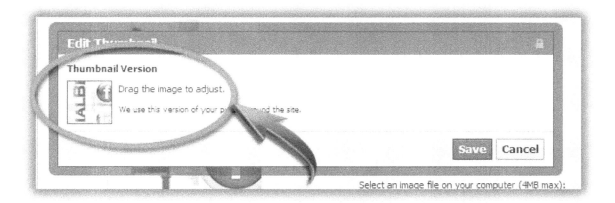

More Profile Picture Examples:
http://www.facebook.com/mdimaging
http://www.facebook.com/martinlevyrealtor
http://www.facebook.com/SouthLakeTahoeVacationRental
http://www.facebook.com/maidbrigadebayarea
http://www.facebook.com/socialbiznow

Day 6: Adding Content

"Be yourself. Above all, let who you are, what you are, what you believe, shine through every sentence you write, every piece you finish."

- John Jakes, American Historical Fiction Author

Your Wall is your opportunity to engage with your visitors. Think of it as a blank canvas where you can create a living, ongoing conversation with your customers - that's a powerful tool in your online marketing toolbox.

Writing on your Wall helps you overcome one of the biggest challenges for your business - how to stay visible in front of your potential customers.

The more you write and share, the more likely you are to build a following and increase the number of "Fans" you have - or those who have "liked" your Page.

The Power of "Like"

The power of social platforms like Facebook is that people choose to listen and follow you, and they are therefore already pre-qualifiying themselves as potential customers, because they're already interested in what you have to say.

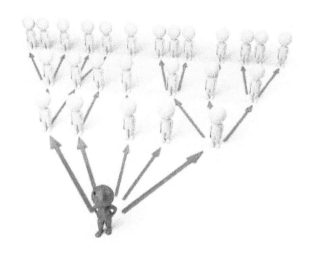

The reason that you want a visitor to your Page to "Like" you is because once they have clicked that "Like" button, your wall posts will now show up on their "Most Recent" or "Top News" wall.

This means that when you post information on your Wall, it is automatically posted to the walls of your fans, giving you much greater visibility, and giving you the opportunity to continue an ongoing relationship with your visitors.

If they like what they see, they might share your posts to their friends, which helps you get even *more* visibility, and the power of "viral" social networks.

So now that you're all set up with a business Page, you need to begin posting content on the Wall.

The Why, Who, When and What of Posting

Why do you have a business Page on Facebook? The "**Why**" is going to determine your content goals, which will in turn help you to define your target visitors, how often you'll post, and even the tone you'll strike on your Page with your visitors.

Begin by defining your objectives. Perhaps it's decreasing the number of customer complaints, increasing the number of new clients, increasing the number of referrals,

increasing traffic to your website, reducing the cost of lead acquisition, increasing the amount of revenue per customer, initiating new product ideas...whatever the reason, this will help define the nature of the content of your posts.

Determining your goals will help you to determine who you are trying to reach, and why.

For example, if you're an organic California Olive Oil company trying to reach increase market share by attracting new tourists to the region, you may post content about what those tourists might be interested in while they're visiting the area.

Next, you could create three or four categories of information that your content can connect back to e.g. local tourist treasures, top area restaurants, how olive oil is made, olive oil recipes.

Social Content Calendar

One of the biggest challenges of social media is in the time commitment.

Researching, creating, writing and editing content is a critical part of marketing your business on Facebook. Managing your time, as well as trying to think of what to write on a regular basis can seem like an enormous challenge.

SOCIALBIZ *Now*
A Real-World Guide to Social Media

If you don't post content on a regular enough basis, your Facebook visitors will soon see that your page isn't active, and stop visiting you. One of the main reasons that you've set up a Facebook business Page is to stay visible in front of potential customers, and if you don't post to your Wall, your information will not be seen in their content stream.

How Often Is Enough?

One of the most common questions about posting on Facebook is "How Often is Enough - or Too Much?"

The answer isn't a simple one.

The real question is "How often will my posts be seen by my visitors?"

If you post too _little_, you defeat the whole purpose of being on Facebook, which is to stay top of mind and visible.

If you post too _much_, you may become annoying, and even end up "Unliked" by visitors.

The answer to this is to create a <u>Social Content Calendar</u>. By setting up a time each day which is dedicated to researching, writing and posting content, you're far more likely to be consistent over time. Consistency is the key to successfully producing quality content, engaging with visitors and gaining traction.

As you create your **<u>Social Content Calendar</u>**, relate each post back to each category.

<u>Use the 2-Week - Social Content Calendar at the end of this Chapter</u> to help you start creating and tracking your posts bi-weekly.

Example of a single post on a Social Content Calendar:

Date	Day	Topic	Post	Posted By
04/18/2011	Monday	Recipes	Choosing a cold-pressed olive oil can be similar to selecting a wine. The flavor of these oils vary considerably and a particular oil may be more suited for a particular dish.	RM

Set up a Schedule

To be successful at building your Facebook community and increasing visibility for your business, you need to set a regular schedule for posting and checking in with what's happening with your Facebook presence and connections.

Establish a routine by dedicating 15-20 minutes twice a day - morning, afternoon or evening, whichever suits your schedule better, to check your Facebook page, post an update, and interact with your community.

Use the Facebook Suggested Activity Checklist at the end of this Chapter as a guide to create your own schedule.

Pre-Schedule Posts

You can also use a tool like Post Planner, a 3rd-party application which lets you pre-schedule posts to your Facebook business Page in advance.

To use Post Planner, go to http://apps.facebook.com/postplanner, and click on the "**Add to My Page**" link.

Give permission to add Post Planner to access your Profile and Pages, and once it's installed, it will display a page like this:

To schedule posts for a future time or date, post your update as you normally would and then select the time and date for when you want the post to appear. You can also have an email sent to you to confirm when your post actually appears by checking the "**email me when it posts**" box.

Topics Outline

Ideas for posting can come from anywhere - news, blogs, emails, customer service, past content, articles, magazines, white papers..

Create a list of Topics to which you can add ideas as you go. The key is to consistently add to your Topics list from anywhere you might find inspiration.

<u>**Use the Facebook Topics Ideas List at the end of this Chapter**</u> as a starting point.

Here are some suggestions for writing Topic ideas:

- Share an experience
- Offer Expert Tips
- Describe a passion
- Invite/Offer an Opinion
- Write a Case Study
- Write a Review
- Give/Ask for advice
- Respond to a News story
- Report a Trend
- Question an Idea
- Quote someone else (with credit)
- Describe a person/place/thing
- Share an Anecdote
- Draw an Analogy
- Narrate a story
- Explain a Process
- Give an Example
- Write a List

- Define a Concept
- Argue a Point
- Write a Speech
- Ask a question
- Post an Event

Assigning Resources

If you aren't doing it yourself, make sure that you assign someone to the responsibility of researching, developing, writing, creating and posting content, according to the Social Content Calendar that's been created.

Make sure someone is responsible for responding to comments, as well as monitoring for comments that are posted.

This means that you need to have guidelines in place to make sure that the person responsible understands and complies with what is and isn't acceptable on your Wall.

Finding Your Writing "Voice"

The goal of publishing content on Facebook is to encourage your visitors to connect with you and become part of your community. As you write, you will begin to develop a writing style that reflects you and what you want people to know about your business.

The style you develop over time becomes your "voice" online, and includes the language, themes, beliefs and passion you put into your content.

The more authentic, real and personal you make your writing style and your content, the higher the level of engagement you'll find.

People like to connect with real people, not corporations or nameless, faceless entities - and the online community can tell very quickly when someone isn't being authentic.

Tip! Your "Fans" will only see some of your wall posts - remember that your posts will be mixed in with all the other posts from other Pages and Friends that each visitor has. You may be one of a few, or one of many, many other posts.

Writing Tips

Here are some simple rules, tips and best practices for posting content on Facebook:

What to Post: the 80/20 Rule
- 80% interesting or informational content
- 20% sales "pitch" - people don't like to be "sold" to, they want to be "attracted" to you by the quality of the content you post

How Often?

- Between 3x a day and 3x a week is ideal, depending on your time commitment and resources for posting
- Don't overdo the number of posts on Facebook, it could clutter your users' newsfeeds and they might be inclined to "un-like" or hide your posts

Engage

- Reply to questions
- Thank visitors for compliments
- Respond to comments
- Pose thoughtful questions and provide content that's valuable

Add variety

- Post photos, videos, links, questions etc. as well as written text to keep it interesting
- Vary the length of your posts, don't make them all one sentence or one paragraph, it will look boring and/or automated

Keep it Simple

- Keep your posts short and to the point, two or three sentences is optimum
- This isn't a place for long paragraphs or dissertations - use your blog for that
- Keep to one point or topic for your post - any more and you'll confuse people
- A well-chosen image may catch more attention than words.

Keep it social

- Be authentic
- Use a "real" voice
- Talk in the first person where you can
- Share and celebrate achievements with your fans
- Ask questions and invite participation
- Talk about…Facebook! (Its' the most popular topic on Facebook!)

Now you're armed with lots of ideas, let's begin by posting to your Wall.

Facebook in 14 Days! A Practical Guide to Get Your Business Online

- 105 -

Post to Your Facebook Wall

Step 1. Go to the Wall

Click on the "**Wall**" link immediately below your Profile Picture to get to your Wall.

At the top of your business Page wall there is a textbox into which you can type a message.

Step 2. Write a comment

The default selected option is "**Status**". Type some text into this box. to share to your Fans. You will also see other options above the textbox, "**Photo**", "**Link**" and "**Video**".

Depending on your interaction with Facebook's features, you may also see other options such as "**Questions**".

Tip! The "**Questions**" option shows up on your Wall only if you've answered a Question posted by someone else using the Facebook Question feature.

Type directly into the "Status" box and click the Share button. Your post will be immediately visible to your Fans.

Tip! If you want to add a **Photo**, **Link** to another website or **Video**, type your written content *first*, then click on one of the other options to add additional content to your post. Your "**Status**" text will be hidden in "**draft**" mode until you've completed adding other content.

Step 2. Attach a Link

You can add more content to your post by adding a hyperlink to an external website (for example another web page or a video on YouTube).

To do this, click the "**Link**" hyperlink above the textbox, and type the link to the content you want to add.

Click the "**Attach**" button, and your comment will appear below the link you've attached.

Step 3. Choose a Thumbnail

If the link you've attached has any thumbnail pictures associated with it, you can choose which thumbnail will show up with your post. Click on the ">" arrow to cycle through the available thumbnails to find the one you want to appear with your post. Check the "**No Thumbnail**" box, if you don't want a picture to appear with your link.

Step 4. Post to the Wall

You're now ready to post your status update, along with the link if you added one, to your Wall. Click the "**Share**" button to post the status update to your Wall. Your text will appear above any other content you've attached.

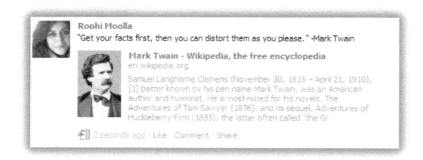

How to Delete a Post

You cannot "**edit**" a post once it's shared, but you **can** delete a post. Note that once you've deleted a post, you cannot restore it. To delete a post, hover over the post you just created, and a small "**x**" and "**Remove Post**" link will appear in the upper-right corner.

Click on "**Remove Post**", confirm in the popup window that you want to remove the post, and the post will be deleted.

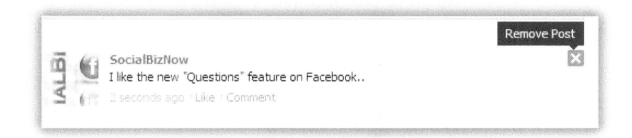

Tip! Facebook also "filters" posts so that the most active posts, for example those with the most comments, show up at the top of a user's **Top News** stream.

Another factor Facebook uses to filter what shows up in the "**Top News**" section is how often that person interacts with you - the more often you interact with someone i.e. comment, tag, share and message someone, the more likely you are to see their posts in the Top News section of your profile.

How to Post to Another Business Page With Your Business Page Profile Name

The default profile that Facebook uses when you post on another business Page is your personal profile, *not* your business page profile. You could be losing opportunities to keep

your business brand visible unless you "switch to using Facebook as a business Page" or you post or comment to other Pages as your business Page profile.

To switch to using Facebook as a business Page, under "**Account**", click on the link "**Use Facebook as Page**", then select the Page to which you want to use. This will "switch" your access and permissions to the Page you select, and you can now post with the Page "persona" instead of your personal "persona".

Select the Page to which you want to switch.

Switch to Page for Individual Posts

If you have a business page on Facebook and you want to show your business brand when posting to other pages without having to "switch to using Facebook as a business", here's a workaround to post to another business page with your business page profile.

Step 1. Select Page Name

On your business wall, type the "@" symbol then start to type the exact name of the page you want to post to. Facebook should recognize the page you're trying to post to, make sure you select the page name if it appears.

Step 2. Share

Type your message and click "**Share**". Your message will post to *your* wall **and** to the page referenced with the @ symbol.

Tip! You must be a friend or fan of the page you want to post to for this to work correctly.

Facebook Posting Tools

Additional tools are available online that can help with scheduling, tracking and posting content.

Here's a brief list of some of the most popular, free tools:

<u>HootSuite</u> - a social media dashboard, for collaboration, schedule updates to Twitter, Facebook, Linkedin, Wordpress and other social networks via web, desktop or mobile platforms plus track campaign results and industry trends to rapidly adjust tactics.

<u>Seesmic</u> - suite of social media management and collaboration tools for businesses and individuals with online applications, mobile devices, and a marketplace of third-party plugins.

<u>SocialOomph</u> - a service that provides free and paid productivity enhancement services for social media users, including automated and scheduled posts and messages.

<u>Amplify</u> - use to auto-post to Twitter, Facebook, Flickr, Google Buzz, Tumblr, Posterous, WordPress and more.

Facebook Topic Ideas List Worksheet

Topic Ideas	Sub-Topics (add your own...)
News / Weather	World, Politics, Government, Reports, Analysis, Editorials, Opinion
Sports/ Fitness / Nutrition / Health	Baseball, Basketball, Football, Hockey, Golf
Business / Marketing / Finance /Sales	Stocks, Economy, Personal Finance, Real Estate, Careers, Small Business
Community / Education /Government	Local, Schools, College, Universities
Entertainment /Music /Movies /Books	Celebrities, Photos, Video, TV
Lifestyles / Recipes /Cooking	Diets, Aging, Health, Beauty
Family /Dating /Relationships	Kids, Parenting, Behavior, Advice,
Technology / Science	Security, Computers, Internet, Games, Mobile, Applications, Innovation
Culture /Travel	Destinations, Deals, Tips, Cruises
Shopping /Reviews	Comparisons, Coupons, Online Shopping
Events	Local, National, Regional, International
[add your own topics]	

Facebook Daily Activity Checklist

Suggested Activity	Complete
Morning Activity	
Check upcoming birthdays, events, post greetings on birthday walls, respond to invites	☐
Check friend/like requests - respond to requests	☐
Check comments, messages, wall posts- respond to inquiries, delete unwanted posts	☐
Create and post status update, including link, photo or video	☐
Evening Activity	
Find and "Like" at least 1-2 new business Pages and/or People, reply to comments on Wall posts	☐
Research online for additional ideas for Topics List and wall post content	☐
Comment on other Facebook business Page wall Posts	☐
Check and track statistics	☐
Post comments on external sites and blogs	☐
[add your own activities]	

2 Week Social Content Calendar Worksheet

Date	Day	Topic	Post	Posted By
Week 1				
	Mon			
	Tue			
	Wed			
	Thur			
	Fri			
	Sat			
	Sun			
Week 2				
	Mon			
	Tue			
	Wed			
	Thur			
	Fri			
	Sat			
	Sun			

Day 7: More About Content

"A picture shows me at a glance what it takes dozens of pages of a book to expound."

- Ivan Turgenev, Russian Author (Fathers and Sons, 1862)

Add Photos

Adding photos and albums to Facebook is a great way to add branding and your business personality to your business Page. You can upload single pictures or create an Album, with collections of photos organized by topic or category.

Think of your products and services and how you could organize them into different buckets of photo categories.

For example, if you're a landscaping company, you could upload pictures of different types of plants for different seasons, plus photos of your clients' gardens. If you're a retail shop, you could upload pictures of your products, organized by product lines.

Tip! Adding visual interest to your Facebook business Page gives you the opportunity to really showcase yourself and stand out above your competitors, many of whom haven't yet realized Facebook's potential.

How To Upload Photos

Step 1. Select Photo Link

Select "Photo" at the top of your home page or profile.

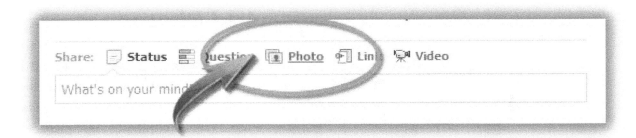

Step 2. Choose an Option

You can either upload one or more Photos from your computer, take a Photo with a Webcam (if you have one installed on your computer) or you can create an album with multiple Photos.

Even if you choose the "**Upload a Photo**" option, you'll have the opportunity to organize your photos later into albums. Select the option to "**Create an Album**".

Step 3. Upload Photos

Click the "**Select Photos**" button in the popup window, then select the photos you want to upload.

To upload multiple photos at once, hold down the Control button on your PC – or the Command button on your Mac – while clicking the image files.

Click "**Open**" once you have selected your photos.

SOCIALBIZ*Now*
A Real-World Guide to Social Media

Step 4. Name the Album

You may see an Uploading window with a progress bar while your photos are being uploaded. You can name your album while you wait for your photos to upload.

After you select photos to upload, you will see a prompt to choose an album name, and set the location for the album and photo quality.

The photo quality for "**Standard**" Facebook photos is usually sufficient for most photos, but if you're a photographer and want to showcase your photos and their quality, you might opt to choose "**High Resolution**".

Step 5. Create Album

A progress bar will indicate the status of your upload. If you've uploaded one or two pictures, the progress bar will disappear very quickly.

Once your photos have finished uploading, and you've named the Album, click the "**Create Album**" button and you'll be directed to the new album, where you can add or edit details to the uploaded photos.

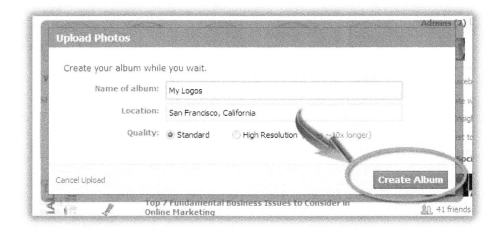

You can also reach the Photos section by clicking on the **Photos"** tab of your business Page.

Select the "**Photos**" link on the left side of your Page below your profile Picture, then click "**Upload Photos**" in the upper right corner.

You can use photo albums to organize your brands, products and services, your portfolios and galleries, staff, success stories, catalogs and any other way you can imagine to showcase your work. Following are screenshots of some great examples of well-leveraged photo albums by companies on Facebook:

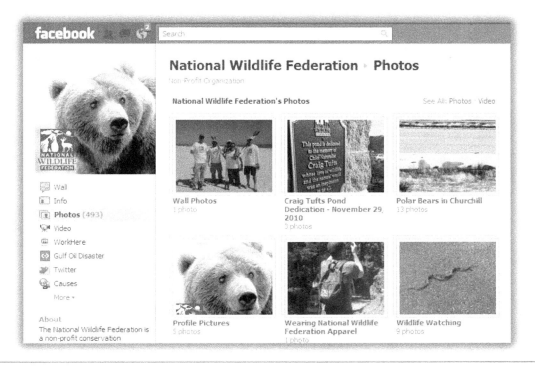

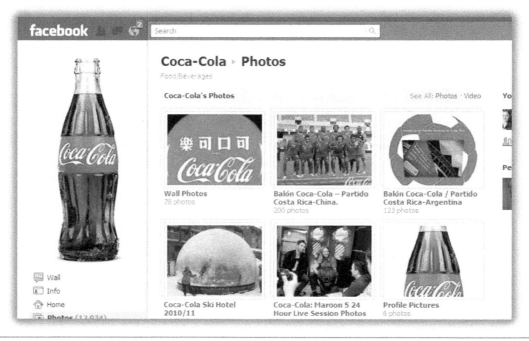

Facebook in 14 Days! A Practical Guide to Get Your Business Online

- 124 -

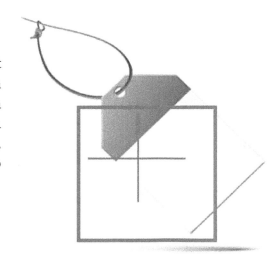

The Art of Tagging

Facebook tagging simply means that you can identify other people in a photo by "tagging" them, or creating a link, on the image. A tag is an area on a photo that becomes an "active hyperlink", and is a hidden visual square that links to the profile of the tagged person.

Tagging Privacy Issues

When you tag someone you are linking to their Facebook Profile - and you are doing so without their prior authorization. Facebook doesn't have any means for someone to authorize a tag before it's posted, other than some specific limits you can set for fans who want to tag photos on your business Page, so use discretion and caution when tagging.

Tip! Tagging someone in a photo will cause the photo to display in the photos section of their profile, and possibly in the top banner photos above their profile, which are the five most recently tagged photos that appear at the top of a person's Wall.

Who Can You Tag?

If you're logged into Facebook as an Administrator of a business Page, you can tag anyone who is a friend of your Personal Profile in photos on that business Page.

If you're logged into Facebook as an Administrator of a business Page, but you've switched to using Facebook as Page, you can only tag a photo with your business Page name.

You can tag any photo you are able to view. If you tag a photo that was not uploaded by a friend, the owner of the photo, as well as the person who was tagged, has the ability to remove the tag.

You can tag with **both** the names of individual people and the names of other business Pages.

 Tip! When you click on a photo to "tag" someone, you can move the square around on the photo by holding down the left-mouse button and moving your mouse.

As a Page Administrator, you can decide whether fans can tag photos of their friends on your business Page, and you can also remove any tags on any photos on your business Page.

Allowing Fans to Post/Tag Photos

Step 1. Edit Settings

There are additional settings for Photos that you can change to decide whether you want to allow Fans to post photos on your Wall or tag photos with your business Profile. To access these settings, login to your business Page the click on "**Edit Page**". From the **Edit Page** section of your business Page, click on "**Go to App**" under the "**Photos**" application section.

Step 2. Additional Permissions

Choose whether you want to allow fans to add photos and/or tag photos, then click the "**Save**" button.

The Top 5 Photos Above your Wall

Whenever a photo is tagged using your business Page name, whether tagged by you or by someone else, it will cause that photo to appear in the top five photos "banner" across the top of your Wall page.

You can tag specific photos to control which photos will appear above your own business Page wall, but you can also "hide" photos that are inadvertently tagged by you, or by someone else. To hide any of the photos at the top of your business Page Wall, click the small "**X**" that appears when you hover over a specific photo.

Facebook Tagging Primer

1. You can only tag friends in photos.

2. You can tag any photo you can view, whether or not you posted that photo, but depending on that friend's privacy settings.

3. You can tag up to 50 people in a photo.

4. If someone un-tags themselves in a photo, you cannot retag them in that photo.

5. If someone's privacy settings prevent tagging, you will not be able to tag someone in a photo.

6. You can remove a tag of yourself in any photo, and this will unlink the photo from your Profile.

7. If you tag someone in a photo that you did not upload, you will not be able to remove or edit the tag. Only the owner of the photo and the tagged user will be able to remove or edit the tag.

8. You can set your notifications so that you will be notified whenever someone tags you, from the Account Settings page.

9. You cannot "approve" a tag of yourself *prior* to being "tagged" in a photo, but you can set your privacy settings so that you're notified of tags, and customize who can see tagged photos of you and remove tags of you.

10. Tagging someone in a photo puts that photo in their top five photos "banner" at the top of their profile.

11. You can tag photos or videos the same way.

12. You can tag comments or posts with

  a. the name of an individual who is a friend

  b. the name of a business you "Like"

  c. a group you belong to

  d. an Application you've used

  e. an Event you're attending

  f. Members of a group you post to or comment in

13. If you tag someone in a comment, it will appear as a link.

14. You can tag multiple people in a post or comment.

SOCIALBIZ*Now*
A Real-World Guide to Social Media

15. Friends who are tagged will be notified that they have been tagged, and a post will appear on their Wall that they have been tagged. They will also receive a notification when someone else comments on a post in which they've been tagged.

How to Tag a Wall Post or Comment

As you type a Wall post or comment, you can "tag" that comment with someone's name, and that person will receive an email message that they've been tagged.

To tag a comment or a Wall post, simply type the "@" symbol before you type the person's name, and the name will become an active hyperlink automatically when you submit the post or comment.

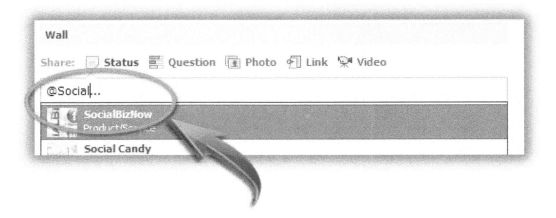

As you type, names that are eligible for tagging (to you) will appear in a dropdown below the text box. Select the name you want, and finish your post.

The name will appear as a hyperlink in your post, and the person or Page Administrator of the Page you tagged will be notified by email that they were tagged.

Photo Tagging Basics

Step 1. How To Tag a Photo

First, find a photo you want to tag, then click the **"Tag Photo"** link. Your cursor will turn into a cross-hair.

SOCIALBIZ*Now*
A Real-World Guide to Social Media

Step 2. Tag the photo

Move the cross-hair cursor over the picture, then click approximately in the center of the area you want to tag, usually over someone's face.

A small square box will appear, as well as a text box into which you can begin to type a name.

As you type, names that are eligible for tagging (to you) will appear in a dropdown below the text box. Select the name you want, and that's it - you've tagged the picture.

To remove a tag, you can do so by clicking the "**remove tag**" link below the picture.

Add Video

"Contrary to public perception, it's not just 'college kids' or 'bleeding edge' internet users who are streaming videos. This creates a fantastic opportunity for advertisers to capitalize on what is now a mainstream audience."

- Erin Hunter, Warrior Cats Author

Video is a great way to connect with your audience, particularly for businesses. By offering the combination of sound, images and even text in an online video, you're creating a much richer experience for visitors to your business Page.

Here are the top eight reasons for posting online videos or "Digital Storytelling" in your Facebook page:

1. *Uses visual, audio and emotional connection*
2. *Easy to view video with broadband access, popular sites include YouTube and Vimeo*

3. *Easy to share, embed and link, easier to "go viral"*
4. *Entertaining - engaging, humor, music, personality*
5. *Real - engaging, enthusiastic, rough, even eccentric can work*
6. *Quick - sometimes easier to convey a message in a video that written or picture*
7. *Fun - for the author and for the viewer - creating a more personal connection*
8. *Cost - very inexpensive to create video these days, camera/equipment cost has dropped*

Video can be used as a stand-alone feature or in addition to other elements of your Facebook Page, but either way, it creates a much more powerful connection to the viewer and therefore elicits a much stronger emotional reaction, giving your visitors a memorable experience.

Video can also enhance your wall posts, be part of a gallery or even used in place of a blog. When you share videos posted by others, you not only give "credit" to other people and help to promote their name (good social media etiquette), but it's also an opportunity for you to offer your own opinion in the "Share" box.

What kinds of videos can you upload about your own business? Anything - within reason(!).

You can upload videos of

- Events/Openings/Celebrations
- Informative/Educational
- Entertainment/Comedy
- Self-expression/Imagination
- Portfolios/Galleries
- Live or Recorded Presentations

Facebook in 14 Days! A Practical Guide to Get Your Business Online

- 133 -

Examples:

Events - http://www.youtube.com/watch?v=kk3TIio1-Uw&playnext=1&videos=tkRw6aX_g8M&feature=featured

Lectures/ Training - http://www.youtube.com/watch?v=ji5_MqicxSo

Entertainment - http://www.youtube.com/watch?v=po0jY4WvCIc

Self expression - http://www.youtube.com/watch?v=nkQuFRfdZow

Presentations - anything you put your mind to.
http://www.readwriteweb.com/archives/top_10_youtube_videos_of_all_time.php

Good vs. Bad Video

What constitutes a good vs. a bad video? Consider the following when creating or sharing a video:

- Visuals - how is the video "framed", is it easy to see, is the lighting sufficient, is the main subject close enough to the camera (but not too close), etc.
- Sounds - can you hear what's being said, is there too much background noise?
- Distractions - is someone doing something in the background that distracts from the main action, either visually or audibly?
- Content - is the main message getting across?
- Connection - does the video make an emotional connection with its intended audience, does it illicit a reaction or response, is there a call to action?

Good - and Not So Good - Video:
http://www.youtube.com/watch?v=DT-DHl8GYAk&feature=related **-** Camera shaking

http://www.youtube.com/watch?v=JtqZjo-EabQ&NR=1 - background noise, subject too far away from camera

http://www.youtube.com/watch?v=p4jv92lbu5g&feature=related - Check your set for background distractions!!

http://www.youtube.com/watch?v=vr3x_RRJdd4 - Free hugs campaign tells a story with music and emotional connection

http://www.youtube.com/watch?v=dMHobHeiRNg - Evolution of dance story - grainy but good!! Humor, eccentric.

http://www.youtube.com/user/charlieissocoollike?blend=1&ob=4 - Charlie McDonnell, good lighting, natural, good editing, no background noise, control of the set, talking to you directly, lots of eye contact, personal energy, easy chatting, personal set, relaxed.

Facebook Default Video Settings

Facebook's default settings are set to "Allow" for visitors to post videos and photos on a business Page, including yours - so check your settings to see what they are and adjust them according to what you want to allow.

Tip! You may be able to post a video on the wall of another business Page, if the business Page allows it. Use caution when posting to someone else's Wall - if you see other videos, it's probably safe to do so.

How To Post a Video to the Wall

To post a video from YouTube or another video site on your own or another person's Wall, follow these steps:

Step 1. Select Wall

Go to the Wall on which you want to post the video (this could be your own Wall, or a friend's Wall).

Click the "**Video**" link above the Share box.

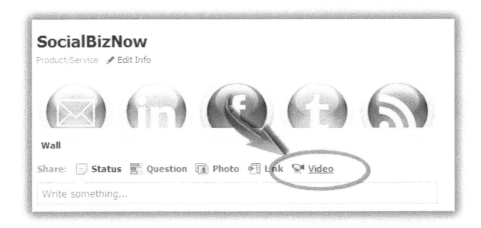

Type a link from an external site into the bar.

Click the "**Upload a Video**" link, then click "**Choose File**" and find a video on your local drive.

Make changes if necessary and click "**Post**" when you are done.

Video Albums

Facebook allows you to upload and manage multiple videos in video albums, similar to photo albums.

You can use video albums to showcase your work, similarly to photos. Ideas to showcase are:

1. **Client Testimonials** - record 30-second video clips of clients (with their permission) endorsing your product or service. Encourage them to say who they are and give the name of their business in the video, so they benefit from the exposure too. You can even allow your customers to post their own videos. A great example of a heavily-used video wall is Coca-cola:

2. **Product features** - if you have a physical product, you can show it in action. Blendtec blenders have taken this to new heights with their "Will It Blend" series of action videos that show their blender in action, and even a dedicated Facebook Page just for the Blendtec video series:

To have a collection of videos as one of your custom tabs, you need to install the **Facebook Video Application** first.

Upload Video into a Photo Album

Step 1. Go to the Wall of your business Page.

Step 2. Click the **"Photos"** link on the left side of the page.

Step 3. Click the **"Videos"** link, then click **"Upload Video"**.

Choose the video file you want to upload from your computer and upload the file. You can also choose to **"Record Video"** to record a video with your webcam.

Follow the on screen directions for your particular upload type.

A successful video upload will generate a "news" story on your Wall, and on your fans' newsfeeds.

Video Privacy Settings

You can choose privacy settings on each video you've uploaded:

Step 1. Select Video - Select a video that you have uploaded.
Step 2. Set Privacy - Click "**Edit this Video**" beneath the video. Choose a setting next to "**Privacy**".
Step 3. Click "**Save**" when you are done.

To control your default privacy settings for videos that have tags of you, click on the "**Privacy Settings**" link under your "**Account**" menu.

In the "Sharing on Facebook" section, click on the "**Customize settings**" link to customize the tag settings for who can see and tag photos and videos of you.

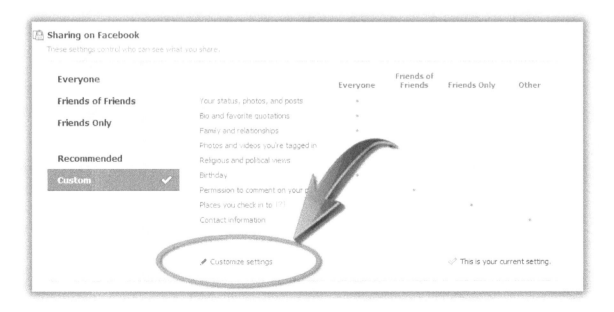

You have several options:

- Everyone
- Friends of friends or
- Friends Only
- Customize

If you'd like to customize these settings even further, in the **Choose Your Privacy Settings > Customize Settings** section, you can select "**Customize**" on any specific setting, and customize your settings even further, including hiding your content from specific people.

Day 8: Create a Custom Tab/ Welcome Page

"Snap judgments are, first of all, enormously quick: they rely on the thinnest slices of experience ... they are also unconscious."

- Malcolm Gladwell, Canadian Author (1963-)

When a user first lands on your business page, are they landing on your business "Wall"? If so, all they're seeing are the last few posts, a couple of comments perhaps – and not much else. It's not very inviting, and definitely not a call to action. It's like inviting a stranger who's passing by to join a conversation that's already in full swing, before even introducing yourself - they don't know who you are or what the conversation is about.

By creating a Welcome Page that introduces who you are and gives your

visitor the opportunity to engage with or "like" you, you're creating the critical "first impression".

This is your "front door" - an opportunity to make an impression and guide your visitor on the action(s) you want them to take, whether it's "liking" your Page, entering a contest, clicking on a link, subscribing to a newsletter etc. - you can do all this with a Custom Page, also known as a Custom Tab.

It's one of the most fundamental things you can do to make your Facebook business page more attractive *and* effective at getting and keeping visitors.

A Tab is simply another "page" within your Facebook "Page" - which is actually a collection of tabs. Your Wall, Info, Photos, etc. are each "tabs" which make up your Facebook profile.

A custom Welcome page with a call to action that's the default landing page can be a very effective tool in increasing the number of "Likes" to your page, as well as give you an opportunity to promote your services, offer special promotions, encourage subscribers and so on.

A custom welcome page can be created in various ways, including custom-coding a page, or creating a tab and simply uploading a graphic.

The easiest way to create a custom welcome page is to use a "Fan Page Editor" - a 3rd-party software application that allows you to create a custom Fan Page like Involver, SocialCandy, ShortStack, Lujure or PageModo.

Each of these applications have free or paid versions, with templates and various documentation that can help you to set up a Welcome Page.

Tip! Each Facebook Fan Page Editor has its own virtues, and issues. Each has also different pricing models, some based on the number of fans, others based on number of pages - so investigate thoroughly before making a decision on which to use.

How a Custom (Fan) Page Editor Works

Fan Page Editors are 3rd-party applications that are web-based software which help you to create custom Facebook pages.

Here are the basic steps involved to use a Fan Page Editor (**FPE**):

1. **Create an account** on a Fan Page Editor application e.g. Involver

2. **Create the content** for the welcome page by using the "building blocks" provided and/or a combination of your own graphics, videos, content etc and "arrange" the content within the Fan Page Editor. You can usually customize various parts of the Page within the FPE, depending on your skill level and the elements available within the FPE.

3. **Connect the application to your Facebook page** by authorizing the application to access your Facebook account

4. **Once authorized, the new application is now "hosting" your content**, and is being displayed on your Facebook page "remotely". This is what's known as an "iFrame" or "framing" content i.e. the content (files, images, forms etc.) is actually not on Facebook, but hosted by the Fan Page Editor.

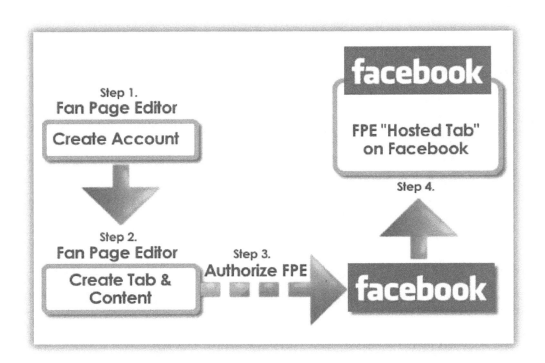

How To Create A Custom Welcome page using Involver

These next steps will walk you through the process of creating a basic custom Welcome Page using Involver.

What you'll need: A customized image or text that you want to use within your Facebook Page as the image or text that your visitors will see when they first land on your Page.

Step 1. Login to your Facebook business Page

You need to be logged in to Facebook because you're going to "connect" Facebook with Involver in just a moment.

Step 2. Go to Involver

Open up a new browser window or tab, and go to http://www.Involver.com/applications

Step 3. Install Static HTML application

Click on the "**Install**" button under **Static HTML**

Step 4. Connect Involver to Facebook

Select the page you want to give access to - this is the business Page to which you want to add a Tab. You may have to give permissions to the Static HTML application to access your Facebook page and/or fill out an information form.

Step 5. Choose Tab Type

You will see three choices:

1. Upload an image *or*

2. Add Custom HTML *or*

3. Use custom SML ("**S**ocial **M**arkup **L**anguage") – a special license is required from Involver as well as some technical knowledge to use this – let's leave this one alone for now.

If you have a web designer who has designed a page for you in HTML, you can select Custom HTML and paste the HTML into the textbox. If not, the easiest option is to select "Custom Image" and upload an image.

Tip! The maximum width for a Fan Page is 520 pixels wide. While there is no maximum height, you may get a vertical scrollbar if you make the height of your Fan Page taller than 800 pixels.

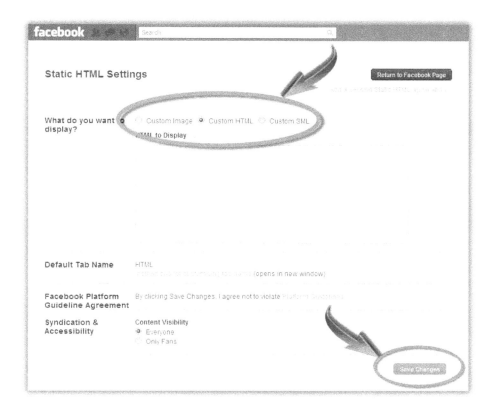

If you want to upload an image, click "**Custom Image**" as the Tab Type, then click "**Browse**" and upload the image.

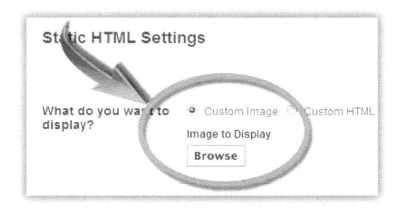

Step 6. Save Changes.

Click "**Save Changes**" to save your changes. If you did this step correctly, you'll see a confirmation message at the top of the screen. Click on the "**Return to your Facebook Page**" button to view your new page.

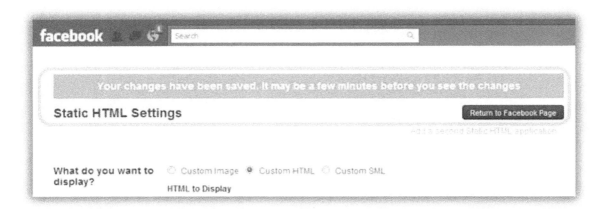

Step 7. Rename Tab

The next step is to rename your new Tab. The default name is "Static HTML" - this isn't useful to a visitor, so choose a name that makes sense and describes the page. For example, if this is going to be the landing page for your business on Facebook. Then you might choose "Welcome" as the name for the Tab.

Click on "**Edit Info**" at the top of your new page, then click on "**Apps**" in the left navigation.

Click on "**Edit Settings**" under the **Static HTML for Pages** application description. This will open a small popup window where you can edit the new Tab name.

Type a new name to describe your new landing page.

Change the name of your new page to describe your new landing page, click "**Save**" AND then click "**Okay**".

Step 8. Set Default Landing Tab

The final step is to set your new page as the default landing page for your Facebook business account. From the top of your business Page, click on the "**Edit Page**" button, then click on "**Manage Permissions**" in the left menu to get to the permissions screen.

Under "**Default Landing Tab**" select the name of your new page from the dropdown.

That's it – congratulations! You've created a custom Facebook Welcome page! You can always edit your page by clicking "**Edit Settings**" at the top of the page – this link is only visible to page administrators.

 Tip! Once you've created a Welcome page, make sure you have a clear call to action like "Like Us", "Subscribe to our Newsletter", "Get a Coupon Code" or "Visit our Website" on the page. A compelling call to action is far more likely to result in a visitor doing what you want them to do, which is interact with your business page before leaving.

The goal here is to get visitors to engage with your Page.

More custom Tab examples
http://www.facebook.com/martinlevyrealtor?v=app_4949752878
http://www.facebook.com/SouthLakeTahoeVacationRental?sk=app_194189853950183
http://www.facebook.com/PlayScreenBocceBall?sk=app_4949752878

 Tip! You can add up to a maximum of 10 custom tabs to a Facebook business Page.

How to Create a Custom Page Reveal

You've seen them everywhere on Facebook - those fancy "**reveals**" that when you "**Like**" a page and become a fan you get to see a special bit of content, maybe a coupon, special offer or other "**fan-only**" cool stuff. And now you want to know how to do this for your own Business Page (without having to buy a Fan Page Editor).

This is what's known as a "**Reveal**" - and is an opportunity for you as a business to "reward" your fans when they land on your business Page. If you're not a fan you see a sign that

says **"Like Us!"**, and as soon as you click the **"Like"** button, the **"fan-only"** content is **"revealed"**.

This is accomplished by installing a simple application into your Facebook page in just a few steps.

This section will walk through the steps of how to **Create a Custom Page Reveal** using an application called **Static HTML,** from a company called Involver.

Earlier in this chapter, you learned how to Create a Custom Business Page using Involver's **Static HTML** application.

If you followed the Create a Custom Business Page tutorial, then you already have **Static HTML** installed, so you can skip the first step and go directly to **Step 2.**

What You'll Need

To create the reveal with this method, you'll need the following:

1. **A Facebook business Page** already set up
2. **Two separate images**: (you can create these with a graphics editor like Microsoft Paint or with help from your graphic designer)

    1. One image will be what only Fans see - so this will be the one with the "revealed" content - perhaps a special offer or coupon.

    2. The other image is what Non-Fans see - the one that says "Like Us!" or something similar, to encourage your visitors to like the Page.

Step 1. Install Static HTML Application

Make sure you're logged into your Facebook business Page.

Click on the **"Edit Page"** button.

Click on "**Apps**" in the left menu.

At the bottom of the list of Installed Apps, click on the " **Browse more applications**" link. This is the Applications directory page.

Type "**static HTML**" into the search box, and hit **Enter** to submit the search form.

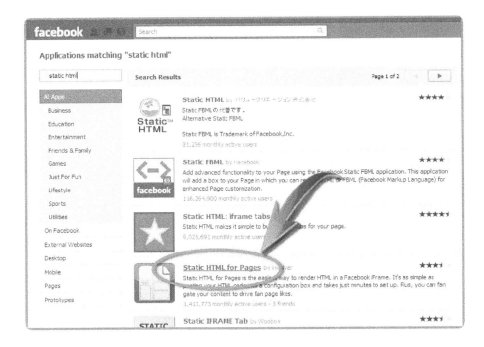

In the search results, you'll see the "**Static HTML for Pages**" (by Involver) link, it should appear as the 4th one down in the results. Make sure you use the Involver application, not another one.

Click on the link "**Static HTML for Pages**", you'll be directed to the application's Facebook page.

On the left menu, click on the "**Add to my Page**" link.

Click the "**Add to Page**" button in the **Add Static HTML for Pages to your Page** popup window, then click "**Close**".

You've now completed the steps to install the **Static HTML application** to your business Page.

Next, we need to add the two images, one for fans, one for Non-fans.

Step 2. Go To App

Navigate back to your business Page (the easiest way from here is to find the Page by typing the name into the search box at the top of the Page). Return to the list of Applications installed for your business Page by clicking on **"Edit Page"**, then **"Apps"** in the left menu.

You will see the **Static HTML** application in the list, click on the **"Go to App"** link.

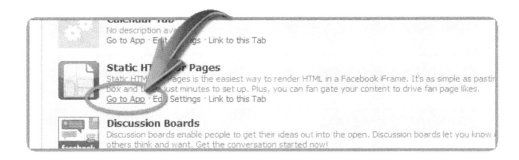

Step 3. Upload FANS ONLY Image

The first image that you want to use initially is the one for **ONLY Fans**. (We'll upload the NON-fan image in Step 4.) On the **Static HTML** settings page, select the "**Custom Image**" option, then click "**Browse**" to find and upload the FAN-ONLY Image you want to display. This image will be the one you are "revealing" *after* the visitor has "liked" the Page.

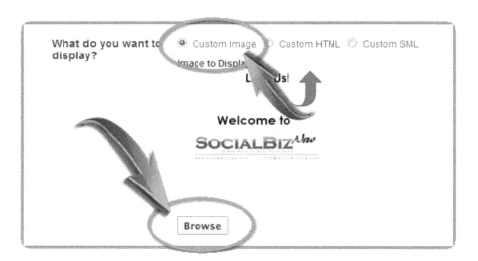

Step 4. Upload NON-FANS and FANS Images

The second image you'll upload is the one for NON-FANS. Under the section "**Syndication & Accessibility**", under "**Content Visibility**", click on "**Only Fans**".

This sets the picture you've just uploaded to be visible to Only Fans.

Now check the box under "**Display Custom Image to Non-Fans**", and you'll see another "**Browse**" button appear after a second.

Click the "**Browse**" button and locate the image you want to appear for NON-FANS.

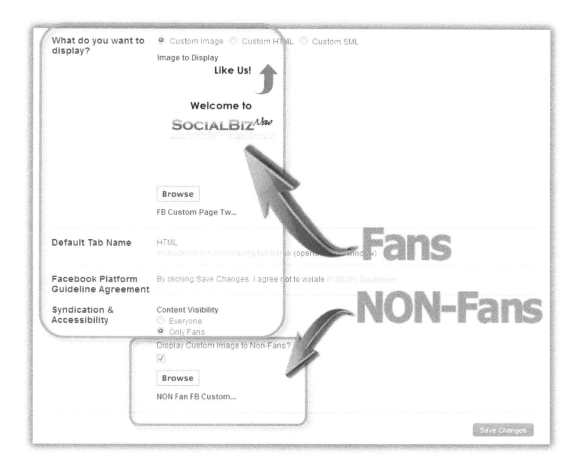

Click the "**Save Changes**" button to save all your changes. You'll see a confirmation message at the top of the screen. Click on the "Return to Facebook Page" button to go back to your business Page.

That's it! You've just completed all the steps to create a Fan/Non-Fan Reveal on your Facebook page.

If you want to test your new "Reveal" and see what a Non-Fan would see, you'll need to ' **Unlike**" your Page first, since you're currently logged in as a Page Administrator.

Click on "**Unlike**" at the bottom of the Page in the left menu and you'll see the Non-Fan view.

Click "**Like**" again to see the page as a Fan.

And here's the final result:

A Non-Fan View of a Custom Page with the hidden "Reveal" :

And the Fan View of the same Custom Page when "revealed":

Day 9: Promote Your Page Part 1: Add Likes and Friends

"I existed from all eternity and, behold, I am here; and I shall exist till the end of time, for my being has no end."

- Khalil Gibran, Lebanese American Poet, Author (1883-1931)

Your business page on Facebook is a great way to promote yourself and your business – and more and more businesses are leveraging opportunities within Facebook to capture "Like"s and engage with their Facebook fans on a new level.

Now that you have a business Page, you need to actively promote it so people know it exists, can find it easily, and can engage with it.

This chapter focuses on several ways you can invite people to your business Page from *within* Facebook, including:

1. **Add a Like Box** to your website/blog
2. **Suggest to Friends** feature
3. **Import Contacts** - from your email client or spreadsheet

Facebook in 14 Days! A Practical Guide to Get Your Business Online

- 161 -

There are also several ways you can immediately start to promote your business Page from *outside* Facebook. including:

1. **Add the "Facebook" icon** to your website/blog with a link back to your Facebook Page
2. **Add a "Like" button** to blog posts
3. **Include a hyperlink** to your Page username/vanity URL in your email signature
4. **Include your Facebook username/vanity URL** in all your offline marketing material, including business cards, brochures, flyers, invoices, posters, coupons, print advertising, billboards, radio and television ads, etc.

Add a "Like" Box to Your Website

You've probably seen the "Like" box on other websites already. It's the Facebook framed "box" where you can see the most recent posts from a Page, how many people including your friends already 'Like" the page, and where you can click the "Like" button without having to go to Facebook itself. This section shows you how to add a "Like" box to your own website, so your website visitors can "Like" your Facebook Page directly from your website.

What You'll Need

In order to complete the following steps, you will need to be able to access your website pages so that you can paste a small snippet of code on a Page.

You can do this with any website or blog that's build with a Content Management System like WordPress, Drupal or Joomla, or any site where you can access the code behind the pages.

The following instructions will walk you through the process of adding a

Like box to a **WordPress** blog, and the steps will be very similar in most cases. If you're not sure, you may need to ask your Web Designer to help you.

Tip! Go straight to the **Facebook Like Box page** here: http://developers.facebook.com/docs/reference/plugins/like-box
Remember to change the **Facebook Page URL** to the Facebook URL for your Facebook business page, so you get the correct code!

Step 1. Copy the Web Address

The first thing we need is to get the **web address** of our business page - we're going to use this later. From your Facebook business Page, **make sure you're on the Wall page**, and copy the **web address** that's in the browser address bar. Paste this address into a Notepad or other temporary document for now.

Step 2. Edit Page

Once you're logged in to your Facebook business Page, click on the "**Edit Page**" button in the upper right corner of the Page.

Step 3. Add Like Box

Click on the **Marketing** Link in the left navigation menu:

Click on "**Add a Like Box to your Website**".

 Tip! A Facebook "**Badge**" is not the same as a "**Like**" box. A "**Badge**" is just a picture that links to your page, whereas a "**Like**" box has a "feed" of your latest posts, with title links and descriptions.

Step 4. Customize "Like" Box

Paste the copied web address from your Page that you collected earlier in the Facebook Page URL textbox, or change the default text *http://www.facebook.com/platform* to *your* business page address.

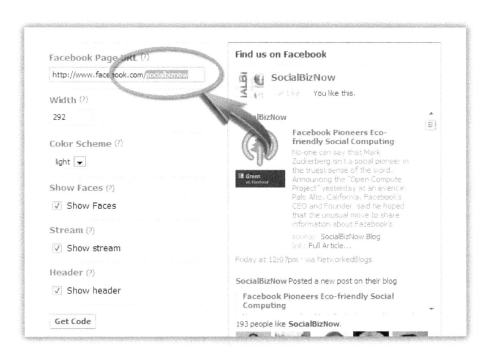

Change the width, color scheme and other form options to see what your "Like" box will look like on your website. "Show stream" means that the posts on your Facebook Wall will show up in the Like box.

Once you're satisfied, click the "**Get Code**" button.

Step 5. Copy Code

Copy the code in the **iframe** or **XFBML** box and paste the code into your website/blog, in the location where you want the Like Box to appear.

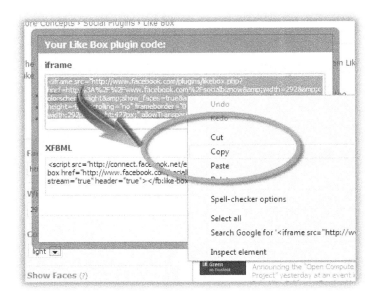

How to Add the Like box to WordPress

For websites and blogs built with **WordPress**, you can add the "**Like**" box to the sidebar or on any Post or Page by using the built-in **Widgets** feature of WordPress. The following additional step shows you how to add the "**Like**" box to the sidebar of your WordPress website/blog:

Step 6. Add Text Widget

Login to your WordPress dashboard, and under the **Appearance** menu, click on "**Widgets**".

Facebook in 14 Days! A Practical Guide to Get Your Business Online

- 166 -

Select the "**Text**" widget from the list of available widgets, and drag the widget to the sidebar or where you want your **Like** box to appear.

Paste the code snippet you copied earlier into the Text box and click the "**Save**" button.

Test to make sure the Like box is appearing correctly on your website.

 Tip! If no posts are showing up in your Like box on your website, try adding a few more posts to your Wall. It sometimes takes a few posts to "activate" Facebook's feed into the Like box.

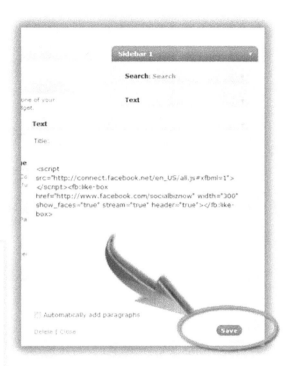

Invite Others

There are a number of ways that you can invite visitors on or off Facebook to your Page to get your page more visibility.

As a Page Administrator, you have the option to suggest your Page to your Personal Profile friends

Step 1. Suggest to Friends

From the business Page for which you are an Administrator, select the "**Suggest to Friends**" link.

From the popup window, click on the names of those you want to invite, and click "**Send Recommendations**" button.

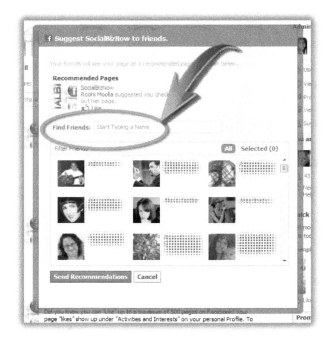

You can find friends to suggest your Page to by typing a Name into the textbox, and you can filter your search by clicking the "Filter Friends" option, which gives you different options by which you can group your Friends, depending on their personal preferences or location.

Your friends will see a "**Recommended Page**" notice on the right-column of their Wall. A preview of what your Friends will see is in the popup window above the Friend selector after you select "**Suggest to Friends.**"

Options for Sharing for Non-Admins

Non-Admins do not have the option to suggest a Page to friends, and are not able to view the "**Suggest to Friends**" link. However, they can share a Page with their friends by clicking the "**Share**" link in the bottom left side of the Page.

A non-Admin can then choose to share the Page via a post on their profile, which may appear in their friends' News Feeds. Non-Admins can also share a Page with specific friends via a direct Message.

Import Contacts

Another way to invite visitors to your Page is to Import Contacts. You can upload a maximum of 5,000 contacts to invite as Fans to your Facebook Page. In order to upload

contacts, you must convert your contact emails into a file that is supported by Facebook's upload process.

Step 1. Go to the Marketing tab

From within your business Page, click on the Marketing link on the left navigation menu.

Step 2. Tell Your Fans

Click on the **"Tell Your Fans"** link to see the Tell Your Fans popup window.

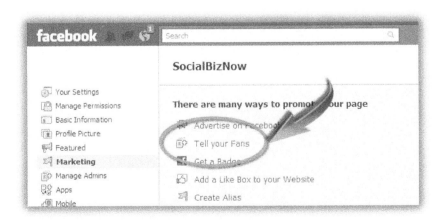

Facebook in 14 Days! A Practical Guide to Get Your Business Online

\- 170 -

Step 3. Upload Contacts

From the popup window that appears, either Choose a File to upload your contacts.

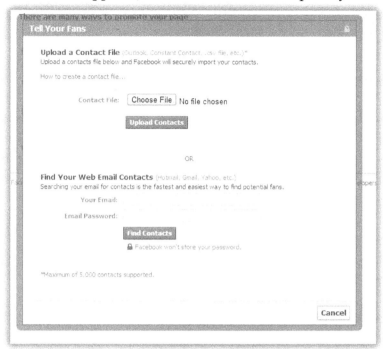

If you don't have a contacts file created yet, you can click on the "**How to create a contact file...**" link, which will show instructions on how to create a contact file for a variety of different email programs.

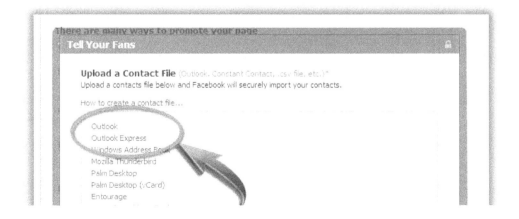

Step 4. Find Email Contacts

Another option is to find contacts via your web email addresses. Facebook gives you this option on the same screen as the "Tell Your Fans" popup window. If you use this option, be aware that Facebook will then "scrape" your web email contact addresses to find your connections, and those people will then be invited to join you on Facebook.

 Tip! Importing existing contacts from your current email lists is a very effective way for you to invite your connections, but it also gives Facebook the opportunity to get more people onto their platform, so just be sure that inviting others onto Facebook is something you want to do before you choose this option.

If they don't already have an account on Facebook, your contacts will need to create an account before they can connect.

 Tip! Giving Facebook access to your email contacts means that Facebook now has those email addresses. Make sure you understand that by giving Facebook those emails, you're doing so without their explicit permission. I recommend that you only invite people to join Facebook that you know, or that you know want to be on Facebook.

Day 10: Promote your Page Part 2: Connect With Twitter

"It's about the things that surround you in the modern world and, just because they're there, shape the way you think and behave; and why they exist in the form they do; and who — or what — was responsible for them existing at all."

- James Burke, Science Historian, Connections

One of the ways you can share content between your social networks is to allow your accounts to connect or "sync" with each other.

On Facebook, you can connect your Twitter account to your Facebook Page so that your "Tweets" automatically appear as Facebook Page posts on your Page Wall.

You can also link your Twitter and Facebook accounts so that your Facebook posts appear as Tweets on Twitter.

This means that you can share information with both your Twitter followers as well as your Facebook fans.

How To Connect With Twitter

There are several different ways you can connect Facebook with Twitter:

Publish FROM Twitter to Facebook

Manually Posting Individual Tweets

You can publish Twitter posts selectively to Facebook using an Application like Selective Tweets that you install to your Facebook Page, and then tagging the Tweet you want to publish with a tag: #fb.

Step 1. Add App to Page

To add the **Selective Tweets** application to your Page, go to the **Selective Tweets** Facebook Page and click on "**Add to My Page**" link.

Tip! The fastest way to get to your business Page is to type your business name into the **Search** bar at the top of any Facebook page. You can also save the Page to a favorites folder or bookmark it in your browser.

In the popup window, add the Page for which you want your Twitter posts to show up by clicking "**Add to Page**", then click the "**Close**" button to close the popup window.

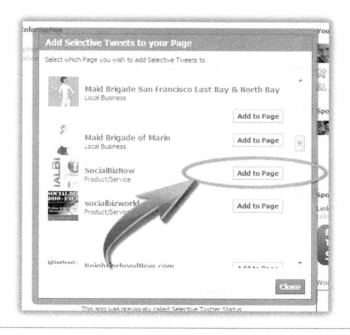

Step 2. Connect Selective Tweets App to Twitter

Return to your business Page within Facebook, then click on "**Edit Page**".

Click on the "**Apps**" link to get to the installed **Apps** screen.

Click on the "**Go to App**" link below the **Selective Tweets** app description.

You'll see **Selective Tweet Status** screen - this is where you can enter the Twitter profile from which you want to post manual tweets to Facebook. Enter the username of the Twitter profile from which you want to post tweets in the **Twitter username** field. Click the "**Grant permission**" link.

You will be prompted to "**Allow**" permission for Selective Tweets application to access your Facebook Page. Click "**Allow**", then click "**Save Changes**".

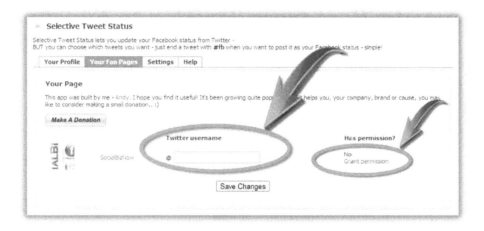

You will now see a confirmation screen for Selective Tweets.

You can now manually post tweets to Facebook from Twitter by adding the tag "**#fb**" (without quotes) to the end of your tweets.

How To Auto-Post from Twitter to Facebook

If you want *all* your Tweets to appear on Facebook, follow these steps to link both accounts:

Step 1. Go to Apps Directory

Login to Facebook and go to your business Page, then click on the "**Edit Page**" button.

Click on the "**Apps**" link in the left navigation menu.

Click on "**Browse more applications**" to get to the Applications Directory Page.

Type "**twitter**" into the search box in the upper left corner of the screen, and hit "**Enter**".

Click on the "**Twitter**" link in the search results to go to the Twitter Application page on Facebook.

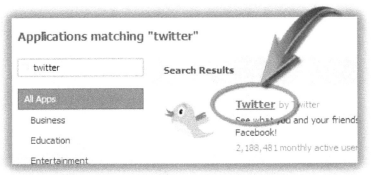

Click on **"Add to My Page"** link in the left menu.

In the popup window, click on **"Add to Page"** next to the Page to which you want to connect with Twitter.

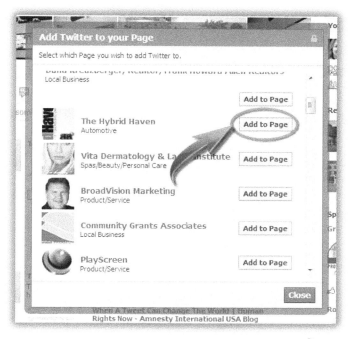

Go to your business Wall, and click on the **"Edit Page"** button, then click on the **"Apps"** link in the left menu. Click on the **"Go to App"** link under the Twitter section.

In a separate browser tab or window, login to Twitter with the account to which you want to connect your Facebook account. You need to be logged in to Twitter so that Facebook will recognize which account you want to connect your business Page to.

Allow the Twitter application to connect to Facebook by clicking the "**Allow**" button.

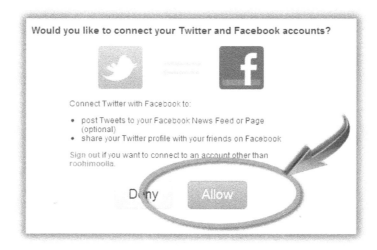

Enter the permissions you want to allow Twitter to access on Facebook. You have the option of allowing Twitter updates to post to your personal Profile, as well as any business Pages you administer. Select the options and the business Page to which you want Twitter to post updates.

Your Twitter updates will now automatically post to your Facebook profile. You can test this by going to your Twitter account and posting an update, then wait a few minutes and see if your Twitter post shows up on your Facebook wall. Look for a post on Facebook with the Twitter icon:

 Tip! You may post different types of content to Twitter or more often than you post to Facebook. Be sure that the kind of content and the frequency of posting is what you want for both Twitter and Facebook if you connect the two.

Day 11: Promote your Page Part 3: Connect Your Blog

"In at least one way we are atypical bloggers. That's because we just keep on posting. The typical blogger, like most people who go on diets and budgets, quits after a few months, weeks, or in many cases, days."

- Stephen J. Dubner, American Journalist, Co-Author:
"Freakonomics: A Rogue Economist Explores the Hidden Side of Everything"

Yes, I know this book is about Facebook, but since we're going to cover the topic of blogging, let's talk about its importance for a moment and the role it plays in your Social Media strategy.

Social Media is simply a conversation – a way to create a communication between the content provider and the end reader to create a mutually benefit relationship through the exchange of information.

Blogging is a tool that provides you with the opportunity to start that conversation with those who are interested in what you have to say. By providing consistent value through high-quality

content over time through your blog, you can build an audience and a community around your blog.

Your business blog should reflect who you are and what you represent - your mission, your values, your business personality, your information and your message.

Why Blog?

A blog is the ongoing dynamic conversation you have with your community. Blogging is an important component of your online marketing strategy for a number of reasons:

1. **Blogging is Inbound Marketing** – it attracts an audience by being a flower (think of the bees you want to attract with honey) rather than a hammer (think of the nail...)
2. **Blogging is extremely Search Engine-friendly (SEO)** – search engines like Google, Bing and Yahoo love blogs because they're dynamic, keyword-rich, content-rich and link-rich
3. **Blogging helps with social networks** – blogs can be connected to multiple other social media tools, applications, networks and websites
4. **Blogging helps with social news sites** – blogs can be connected, distributed and read through RSS feeders and readers
5. **Blogging is permission-centric** – based on the concept that only those who are interested in the content will read your blog, giving you 'permission' to have your voice heard

You can connect your Blog to Facebook so that when you post a blog on your website, the title and brief summary will *automatically* appear on your Facebook wall.

There are several benefits to doing this:

- It effectively syndicates your content so more people see your blog
- It gives your Facebook fans the opportunity to easily share your blog (via the "**Share**" link) to their Facebook friends

---

- It lets more people like and comment on your blog via the Facebook "**Like**" and "**Comment**" links

Here's what a blog post looks like on Facebook, automatically posting from the SocialBizNow blog via **Networked Blogs**:

Connect Your Blog to Facebook

To connect your blog to Facebook, you need to add an application to your Facebook business Page. The application we're going to use for this section is called <u>Networked Blogs</u>**,** a third-party application that will creates the bridge between your blog and your Facebook Page.

There are other applications you can use to connect your blog to Facebook, but **Networked Blogs** is one of the easiest to use. Follow these steps to have your blog posts *automatically* post to your business Page:

Step 1. Go to Apps

Login to Facebook and go to your business Page, then click on the "**Edit Page**" button.

Click on the "**Apps**" link in the left navigation menu.

Step 2. Add Networked Blogs

At the bottom of the "Added Apps" screen, click the link "**Browse more applications**".

Type "**networked blogs**" into the search box in the upper left corner of the screen, and hit "Enter".

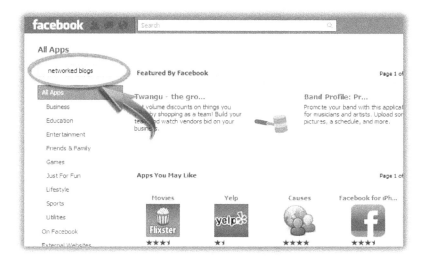

Click the "**Networked Blogs**" logo or link to go **Networked Blogs'** Facebook page.

Click the "**Add to My Page**" link in the left navigation menu of the Networked Blog page.

Step 3. Add to Page

In the popup window that appears, click the "**Add to Page**" button next to the business Page for which you want to add the blog. **Note:** If you administer more than one Page, you'll see a list of pages in the popup Window.

Click the "**Close**" button to close the popup window, and return to your business Page.

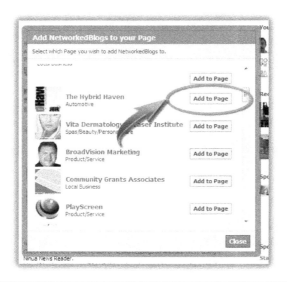

Click on the Networked Blogs "**Blog**" icon in your list of tabs below your profile picture.

Step 4. Register your blog

Click on the "**click here to add it**" link to register your blog on the Networked Blogs application.

On the **Register a New Blog** screen, complete the fields on the form, then click "**Next**".

Click on the "**YES**" button to confirm that you are the Author of the blog that you are adding to your Page.

Tip! If you're not the Author of a blog you want to add, you can still add the blog, you just need to identify the Blog Author on the next screen.

Step 6. Verify Ownership

If you're the Author of the blog you're adding, **Networked Blogs** will ask you to verify ownership.

This is to ensure that you're not claiming authorship for a blog that you don't actually control. You have two choices of verification:

1. **Ask friends to verify you** - this option will send an email to the friends you select (up to 16), and ask them to verify that you are the author of the blog you're claiming.

2. **Use a widget** (a small piece of code that you embed in your website). This option allows you to verify ownership immediately, but you need to have access to your website, either through a CMS system like WordPress or be comfortable with adding the widget code manually to your site.

If you're not comfortable with copying and pasting a small piece of code into your blog, use the first method of asking your friends to verify you.

If you are comfortable with copying and pasting, and you have access to your blog via WordPress or a similar blogging platform, use the following steps to complete the verification process for Networked Blogs.

The next steps will assume that your blog in on a self-hosted WordPress platform.

Step 7. Install Widget to verify Ownership

Click the "**Use widget to verify ownership**" link. You will now see two options, "**Install Widget>>**" and "**Install Badge>>**".

Option 1. Install Widget

If your blog *is self-hosted* using Blogger, or installed via WordPress on a service like Bluehost, then use the option to "Install Widget".

Option 2. Install Badge

If your blog is hosted by a site like WordPress.com i.e. your blog address looks like this http://yoursite.wordpress.com, use the "**Install Badge**" option.

Copy the code that appears in the textbox and click the relevant "**Instructions for...**" link, based on your blog platform.

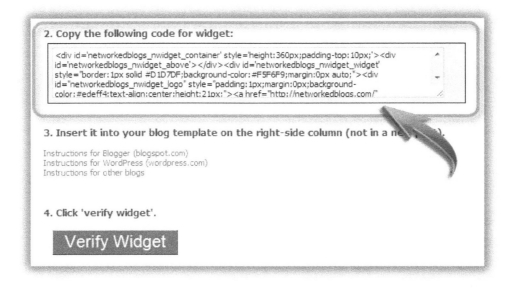

Open up another browser tab or window, and login to your WordPress blog account.

On the **Dashboard**, click on "**Appearance**", then "**Widgets**" in the left menu.

Add a "**Text**" widget to your sidebar, and paste the copied text into the text area, then click "**Save**".

You can remove the widget after it's been verified, so don't worry about the formatting or location of the Text widget, unless you want to keep it on your blog.

Go back to the application page you had open on Facebook, and click "**Verify Widget**".

If you've installed the widget successfully, you'll see a "**Verification successful**" message. Click the "**Next**" button.

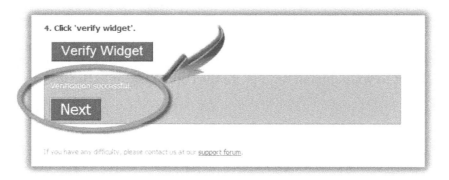

Step 8. Set up Syndication

Now that you've verified the widget, you need to setup Syndication for the blog. This simply means that the blog will be authorized to post to your Facebook business profile. Click on the "**Set up Syndication**" button.

From the **Syndication Settings** screen, click on the "Add Facebook Target" link. This will enable the blog you've just verified to link to your Facebook Page.

Click the "**add**" link next to the business Page to which you want to add the blog. **Note:** If you have more than one business Page, you'll see a list of pages to which you can add the blog.

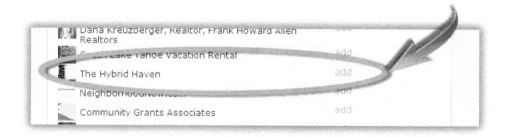

Close the popup window.

You will see a confirmation screen with the name of your business Profile. To edit details, remove the blog link to this Page, or Publish a Test for this blog, hover over the blue bar and click on the "**expand for details**" link that appears.

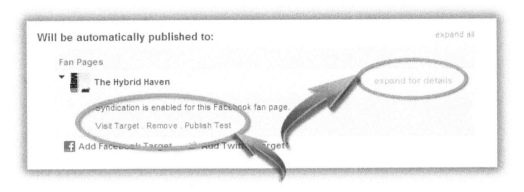

Click on the "**Visit Target**" link to return to your business Page, then click the "**Blog**" link in the left navigation menu to view the Blog. If the blog doesn't appear on the page, and you still see the "**No Blogs Found**" message, click on the "**Click here to verify your settings**" link.

Check the box(es) where you want the blog to appear, then click the "**Click here**" link to grant permission to allow publishing to the fan page.

In the popup window, click "**Allow**" to allow the **Networked Blogs** application to access to post to your business Wall.

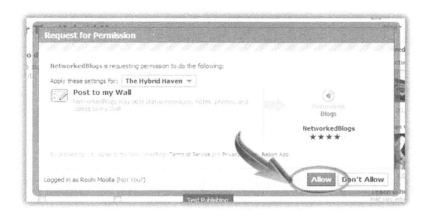

Click the "**Test Publishing**" button to make sure the blog is posting correctly.

You will see a green bar with a confirmation that your settings have been saved. Click on your Page name link that takes you back to your business Page so you can see the test message on your Page Wall.

You should see a message posted on your Page Wall similar to the screenshot below, which confirms that your blog is now posting automatically to your Page Wall. When you write a new post on your blogging platform, Networked Blogs will pull the title of the post plus a brief summary and post it automatically on your Facebook Wall.

And that's it! Your blog is now posting automatically to Facebook!

The number of followers you have on your blog determines how often your blog posts are pulled and posted on your Facebook page.

The more followers you have, the more often your blog posts are pulled. The amount of time varies between 10 minutes and 12 hours.

The average amount of time is about 3 hours delay between the time your blog is posted and when it will appear on Facebook.

Day 12: Promote Your Page Part 4: Facebook Ads

"A good basic selling idea, involvement and relevancy, of course, are as important as ever, but in the advertising din of today, unless you make yourself noticed and believed, you ain't got nothin'."

- Leo Burnett, Advertising Executive (1891-1971), named one of the 100 most influential people of the 20th century by TIME magazine

Facebook is a wealth of demographic and psychographic information - a goldmine for marketers, and one of the primary reasons businesses are flocking to Facebook in droves.

Facebook Advertising are ads that people and businesses purchase and that appears in various places and in different formats throughout Facebook.

A Marketer's Dream: Personalized Ads

Facebook's advertising is customized to a user's interests, friends, preferences and experiences - which means that what you see advertised will be different from what I see.

For example, a student in New York whose interests on Facebook include rock bands and whose friends like Broadway shows might see advertising on a new music CD or band playing a gig in Manhattan while a business owner in San Francisco whose friends like sailing and who "likes" pages on the wine industry might see ads for sailboats, and advertising about limousine rides to Napa wineries.

Facebook tailors and displays the advertising you see according to your interests and those of your friends - it's a granular, customized experience - and a marketer's dream.

Why? Because people are far more likely to trust people they know and recognize, and to engage in things that interest them.

You're much more likely to interact or click on advertising if it fits your interests or you see that one of your friends "liked" the product or service because it's part of your social "sphere" of activity.

How does that help you? As a business, you can leverage Facebook ads to reach a specific demographic or target market, based on geography, interests and demographics.

These are all elements that people share about themselves on Facebook - their preferences are as well as the relationships they have.

Facebook Advertising is one of the key strategies you can implement to get more visibility to your Facebook page.

Sponsored Ads on Personal Profile Wall

Sponsored Ads on Business Page Wall

Facebook Advertising appears in the right-hand column of the screen as either Sponsored Stories or Facebook Ads.

Ads can also appear on many other types of pages including Application pages and Groups.

Ads can be targeted by location, sex, age, keyword, relationship status, job title, workplace, or college.

Buying Facebook Advertising

Costs and Placement

There is no set cost for Facebook Ads, it's based on a bidding or "auction" system which means that you are bidding for advertising space based on your target selections. If you'd like to see what we recommend you bid for each click (CPC) or thousand impressions (CPM), just enter your targeting criteria and go through to Step 4 of ad creation (you won't have to enter any payment information until the next step, so you can do this without purchasing an ad). The "bid estimator" will show you the range of bids that are currently winning the auction among ads similar to yours.

How does Facebook choose which ads to Display?

Facebook's ad system uses algorithms which estimate the best performing ad based on a variety of factors, including the historical performance of the ad and its bid. The bid that's necessary to win an auction fluctuates as the Facebook ad system adjusts to the ads that have been placed, their actual performance, and the pool of competing ads which also changes over time.

In order to stay competitive, you need to monitor your ad's bid over time. If other people place ads with similar target markets but with higher bids than yours, it's possible for your bid to fall below the range of the recommended bid pricing, and if it falls significantly below the range, your ad may stop running entirely.

It's important to try varying ad creatives and targets to keep ads fresh and to test the results of each ad - you may see a better or worse result depending on the text, image or combination of both.

Ad Types

Facebook has two types of Ads: "Stories" and "Ads".

Ad Type 1: Sponsored Stories

A Sponsored Story allows you to publicize either "**Likes**" or "**Posts**" as a type of Facebook advertisement:

Page Like Story: When someone "likes" your page, the "like" will be seen as a "Story" in the right-had column on Facebook - allowing you to promoted your brand by capitalizing on the recommendations that naturally occur within Facebook.

For example, if a friend of yours "likes" a Page, you will potentially see that "like" in your News feed in addition to seeing the same news story on the right-hand column on Facebook.

Page Post Story: A Page Post Story occurs when you post an update to your Wall, and will appear on the right-hand column for users that have liked your Page.

The content for both Page Like Stories and Page Post Stories is automatically generated by Facebook, you don't have the option to modify the content.

When a user clicks on a Sponsored Ad story, it also automatically creates a story on the user's profile page, and may appear on their friends' News Feeds, which gives you even greater visibility.

Ad Type 1: Facebook Ads

A Facebook Ad is an Ad with content that you have control over, where you can type your own text and upload a picture, and the title of which can be a hyperlink to either an external website, a Facebook business Page or specific Tab on that Page.

Facebook Ads for Pages and Events allow users to engage with ads the same way they interact with other content on Facebook, without leaving the page they are viewing. Ads for Pages include a "**Like**" link, while Ads for Facebook Events include an "**RSVP**" link.

Users who see these types of ads can click on these links and by doing so, directly connect with your Pages and Events from the ad itself.

Create an Ad

To begin creating a Facebook Ad, go to your business Page and click on **"Edit Page"**.

Step 1. Go to Create An Ad

Go to the **Ads Manager dashboard** and click on "**Advertise on Facebook**".

You can also select what type of Ad you want: a Sponsored Story or a standard Facebook Ad.

Step 2: Design Your Ad and Choose Ad Type

The first step to creating an ad is to design the Ad. You can select different destinations for your Ad, either a website outside Facebook, or Pages and Applications that you administer within Facebook.

Step 3: Targeting

Targeting allows you to filter the types of Facebook users who will see your Ad. You can target a specific segment of your market by selecting filters such as Geography, Age, Gender, Interests, Connections, Relationship, Education and Work.

The Interests section provides even more detailed targeting filters. These are the filters that Facebook collects based on the information that Facebook users input in their interactions with the platform.

You can toggle back and forth between detailed "**Precise Interests**" and "**Broad Category Marketing**" depending on whether you want to target a very specific group of users or use more general filters across broader categories.

Click on the link **"Switch to Broad Category Targeting" to see the broad category filters.**

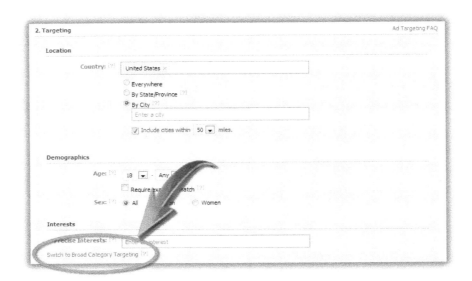

Step 4: Bidding, Pricing & Scheduling

You can choose to pay for your Ad either by the number of **Impressions** or the number of **Clicks**.

Tip! An ad is considered to served as an "**Impression**" every time it's displayed to a visitor, so if one user sees an Ad on their Wall three separate times, that's three impressions. If three different users each see the Ad once, that's also three impressions. A click is when someone clicks on a link in the Ad.

When you pay for **Impressions**, you are bidding on the maximum amount you're willing to pay per **1000** impressions (also known as **CPM = Cost per Mille**).

If you opt to pay for **Clicks (CPC = Cost per Click)**, you are bidding on the maximum amount you are willing to pay each time someone clicks on your Ad.

CPC or CPM?

Your advertising goal will determine whether you choose a **CPC** (cost per click) or **CPM** (cost per thousand) ad type.

- **When to use CPC** - If your goal is to have people click through to your website or your Facebook Page, Event, or Application, then select the CPC option, because your goal is to drive traffic to a specific destination.

With CPC advertising, you can control the actual cost to drive each person to your site. In particular, if you are hoping to drive online conversions through their ads e.g. sales of t-shirts or subscribers to a newsletter, choose the CPC model.

- **When to use CPM** - If your goal is to increase brand, product or service awareness, choose **CPM** advertising (cost per thousand impressions).

When placing bids for your Ads, Facebook only charges the amount required to win the Ad auction. This might be less than the amount you bid.

You can set a **Daily Budget** which limits the amount that you are charged for that ad per day.

As you make selections for your Ad, you'll notice the "Estimated Reach" box on the right side of the screen change accordingly.

Facebook Ad Management

You can use the Facebook Ads Manager to manage multiple Ads and Campaigns, as well as view Reports and manage your Ads Account. To get to the **Ads Manager dashboard**, login to your Facebook account, then type the following web address in your browser: *http://www.facebook.com/ads/manage*.

 Tip! Other than US Dollars, Facebook offers support for paying for Ads in multiple currencies, including Australian, Canadian and Hong Kong Dollars, the British Pound, the Euro, the Japanese Yen and others. Click here for a complete list of acceptable currencies.

You can get to the Ads Manager from the main menu of your personal Profile by clicking on **"Ads and Pages"**.

From within the **Ads Manager dashboard**, you can edit and preview your Ads, see what your Ad would look like on a Profile, check if your ad is running or if your bid has dropped below the .recommended bid, Manage Settings, view and download Reports and check the status of each campaign.

Access and view traffic (visitors/likes/feedback) reports on Pages you administer from the **Insights** link.

Preview a snapshot of what your Ad would look like on a user's Wall by clicking on the "View on Profile" button.

Multiple Administrators

You can set multiple Administrators for your advertising accounts, whether or not they have a Facebook account.

To give permission to someone to be an Administrator on an Ad account you manage, go to the Facebook Ads Manager dashboard. , then click on the "**Settings**" link.

On the "**Settings**" screen, in the section titled "**Permissions**", click on the "**Add User**" button.

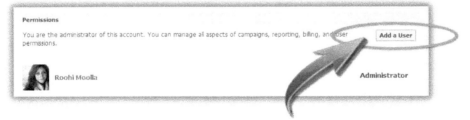

The person will be able to see only the Accounts for which they've been given permission, through their own Facebook Ads dashboard, which they access with their own account.

Use the Facebook Ad Worksheet at the end of this Chapter to gather and record information about each Facebook Ad you place.

SOCIALBiz*Now*
A Real-World Guide to Social Media

Facebook Ad Worksheet

Business Name:	
Date:	
Prepared by:	

General Information

Ad Name/Title	
Destination/Landing Page (URL)	
Ad Type	Sponsored Story_____ Facebook Ad_____
Ad Text	
Ad Image (Description and/or URL to file)	

Demographics

Geography	
Age	
Gender	
Interests	
Keywords	

Bidding and Scheduling

Daily Budget	
Maximum Bid	
Start Date	
End Date	
Payment Type	Pay for Impressions _____ Pay per Click _____

Day 13: Promote Your Page Part 5: Advanced Strategies

"Business today consists in persuading crowds."

- T.S. Eliot, American Author (1888-1965)

Advanced Facebook promotion strategies like contests, giveaways, crowd-sourcing and fostering user-generating content can help take your Facebook business Page to another level.

Building online marketing campaigns around your business Page can help you generate leads, increase visibility, focus and/or expand your target market and help build brand awareness.

These types of strategies are successful because :

- You Create Engagement

- You Encourage Viral Evangelism

- You Build Community

- You Foster Loyalty

- You Drive Ecommerce and Retail Traffic

- You Control Participation

- You Grow your Customer database

Platforms

Facebook has very strict <u>rules</u> on running contests, promotions, competitions and sweepstakes on its platform. While many Facebook users aren't aware of the rules (and in some cases even ignore them) , if you don't abide by its' rules you're taking the risk of having Facebook shut down your business Page completely - which would result in the loss of all your content, relationships and effort.

Rather than take that risk, it's worth investing in a third-party contest platform which allows you to run your contest and are designed specifically to integrate with Facebook so you abide by Facebook's rules at the same time.

Some of the most popular contest platforms are:

- <u>WildFire</u> - offers 10 different promotion types including Sweepstakes, user-generated contests, product giveaways, coupons, quizzes and trivia. Pricing is a flat fee plus a per day fee. For example: If your contest runs for 30 days, the cost is $$25 plus $2.99 per day, for a total of $114.70.

- **Votigo** - some of the biggest brand names have used Votigo including Coca-Cola, KFC, AOL, Dell, Sears, Amtrak, Southwest Airlines, Ford and Intel. There's no pricing given on the website, you have to contact them for a quote.

- **ContextOptional** - provides enterprise-level "social marketing solutions" that build, manage, monitor and measure brand presence across the social web, including "Cause Marketing" for Non-Profits. No pricing given online, this is a customized solution for larger companies and organizations.

- **Friend2Friend** - offers a library of social media applications, including Pages, Contests and Sweepstakes, Media and Promotion, and Analytics. No pricing online.

- **BuddyMedia** - claims "Eight of the world's top ten brands drive their business on Facebook with the Buddy Media Platform", offers ways grow your fan-base, encourage sharing, drive Fans to your website, monitoring tools and content update tools. You can also launch global and local fan Pages. No pricing online.

Promotion Strategy Examples

Large brands and companies like Coca-Cola, KFC, AOL, Dell, Sears, Amtrak, Southwest Airlines, Ford and Intel have been leveraging these kinds of promotion strategies to grow their fan base extremely successfully.

There are a lot of different types of strategies, and in this Chapter we'll take a look at some of the promotion types that are available and provide an example of each strategy in action.

Business: Tribeca Film Festival
Promotion Type: "Like Us" Reveal
Purpose: "Like Our Page" to access videos and other exclusive content

Business: Seattle's Best Coffee
Promotion Type: Giveaway
Purpose: The "Brew-Lanthropy Project" gives away coffee to non-profits suggested by its Facebook visitors

Business: Tornado

Promotion Type: Crowd-sourcing

Purpose: Tornado's Flavor challenge asked its Facebook Fans to generate ideas for its next product flavor

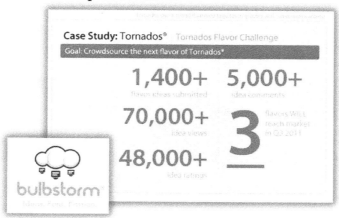

Business: American Express/1-800 Flowers

Promotion Type: Special Offer

Purpose: American Express offers co-promotion with 1-800 Flowers for discount with promotion code on its for Facebook fans

Business:	Tribeca Film Festival
Promotion Type:	Poll/Online Survey
Purpose:	Facebook fans pick a Heineken Award Winner

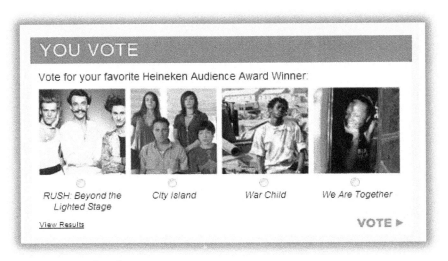

Business:	Starbucks
Promotion Type:	Jobs Board
Purpose:	Online employee recruitment

Business: Tribeca Film Festival

Promotion Type: Quiz

Purpose: a Trivia Quiz to engage, entertain and educate Fans

Business: Mariah Carey

Promotion Type: Featured Songs and Tour Calendar

Purpose: Facebook fans listen to music online and stay current with Tour dates

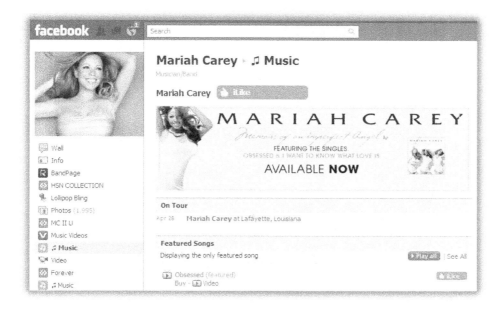

Business: (RED)
Promotion Type: eCommerce - shopping
Purpose: provide visitors with online shopping opportunity directly on
Facebook

Business: Pepsi Max
Promotion Type: Bonus Content and Advertising, Sweepstakes
Purpose: Offers visitors opportunity to enter contest and see bonus videos

Day 14: Metrics

"The most serious mistakes are not being made as a result of wrong answers. The truly dangerous thing is asking the wrong question"

- Peter Drucker, Social Ecologist (1909 - 2005), coined the term "knowledge worker"

Evaluating the success and assessing the impact of your Facebook business Page is crucial to ensuring that you're making decisions based on facts and figures, rather than theory and guesses. As an organization, it's essential to objectively measure and assess opportunities against expenditures and compare results based on efficiency and effectiveness.

What are Metrics?

Metrics are the measurement of the performance of your Facebook business Page. Measuring various factors of your Page will help you gain insight and determine the success of your Page, and what you may need to do to adjust it.

SOCIALBiz *Now*
A Real-World Guide to Social Media

Purpose of Metrics

The main purpose is to consider the cost of your investment on your Page - which is the Return On your Investment (**ROI**) of the three major investments you make to create, manage and maintain your Page:

- o Time
- o Money
- o Resources

You need a solid understanding of the effort you've invested in each of these three areas, as well as a clear picture of the outcomes of your efforts so that you can determine whether your efforts are worth the investment, and where you need to adjust.

To get an accurate estimate of your ROI, , you need to analyze your business Page on Investment vs. Results.

Investment (or Cost) includes:

- o Unit Cost
- o Cost per Customer
- o Support and Maintenance Costs
- o Research Costs
- o Time/Opportunity Costs
- o Service Costs (training, consulting etc.)
- o Software/Hardware Costs
- o Sales Costs
- o Revenue per Customer
- o **Lifetime Value of a Customer**

Let's look at one of the most important calculations when considering the cost or investment in any effort that you undertake for your business: the actual Value of a Customer.

Lifetime Value of a Customer

Do you know how much a customer is really worth to your business?

Many small businesses think of their customers as one-time, single purchase customers. But not only do you generate more revenue from a customer who buys your product more than once, you've also reduced the cost of acquiring that customer, since you didn't have to work as hard for the second sale. In addition, if that customer is happy, they could also potentially be an evangelist of your products, and tell their friends.

Nurturing repeat customers by creating personalized experiences and building ongoing relationships leads to greater lead generation and higher customer retention rates.

It's one of the reasons that social media is so appealing to marketers – it gives business the opportunity to connect and engage with customers and build ongoing relationships through other marketing channels that were previously unavailable.

Add to that the fact that social media has the potential to dramatically reduce the cost of acquiring a customer, and you can see why social media is so appealing to so many.

So let's get back to the actual Lifetime Value of a Customer (**LTV**).

LTV Calculation

A customer that does business with you more than once has increased their value to your business than one who you never see again.

LTV can be calculated using the total value of purchases that a customer makes over the period that customer stays with the business.

Let's look at an example:

=====================================
John buys his first product from Company ABC for $50 in March.

John returns and buys another product from Company ABC in November, for $100.

The total value of John the Customer to Company ABC for a period of one year is $150 ($50+$100).

If the average length of time that Company ABC retains its customers is about 3 years, then the actual value of a customer to Company ABC is

3 years x $150 = $450
==================================
Now that we know the average lifetime value of a customer, we can use this as a measure against the actual Cost to Acquire a Customer (CAC).

The cost to acquire a customer includes labor, marketing, advertising, and sales service costs – and will vary based on your business. But you should be able to calculate this number fairly easily.

Let's look at Company ABC again.

If Company ABC spends $10,000 on its marketing efforts over a period of one year, and gains 40 customers (not leads, actual paying customers), then the cost to acquire is

$10,000 / 40 = $250

The cost to keep a customer, once acquired should also be factored in here, since it is usually significantly less than the cost to acquire a customer – but let's just keep our calculation simple for now.

Once you know how much it costs to acquire a customer, you can determine an estimated Return On your Investment (ROI).

The ROI for any business is fundamental to determining pricing, feasibility and how to respond to market conditions, and a even whether it's realistic to start or stay in business.

Subtract the CAC from the LTV to find the net ROI:

$450 – $250 = $200

$200 is the actual return on investment for Company ABC for a single customer.

At this point, it's important to determine the cost to keep the customer, as well actual costs for running the business.

As you can see, understanding the real numbers that drive your business is critical to its financial success.

Your budget analysis will help you to decide how much you can or should spend on your online marketing efforts.

Use the **Lifetime Value of a Customer Worksheet** at the end of this Chapter to calculate the real value of a customer for your business.

The Power of Engagement

"**Engagement**" describes the actions and events that relate to your Page, and one of the key metrics that you need to measure because it offers key insights into the effectiveness of your Page. Engagement is measured by interaction and activity any time a visitor takes an action on your Page, including "liking", commenting, having conversations, tagging, sharing, sending, and messaging.

Stephen Powers, a Forrester Research Analyst published a paper in 2010 called "**The Online Customer Engagement Software Ecosystem**", where he says that the issue of engagement is becoming more critical for organizations:

"The uncertain economy has increased pressure on companies to engage customers more efficiently, especially via online channels that offer lower-cost ways to interact with customers, enable better lead generation and increase customer retention rates. "

The level of engagement on your Facebook business Page is a critical benchmark in measuring it's success.

SOCIALBIZ*Now*
A Real-World Guide to Social Media

Key Facebook Metrics

There are four key Facebook Metrics you should track to gauge how your business Page is performing:

1. Fans/Likes/Users
2. Page/Tab Views
3. Content
4. Engagement

Tip! To see statistics on any of the above metrics, go to your business Page, click on the **Edit Page** link to go to your business Page Administration Dashboard, then click the "**Insights**" link. From there, follow the instructions below for each metric below.

1. Fans/Likes/Visits

The number of fans you have, or people who "like" your Page, while not the only important metric, can give you a strong indication of whether your Page is continuing to increase its visibility across its target market.

Metrics on Fans include:

- **# of New Page "Likes"** - the number of new people who have "Liked" your Page in a given timeframe

- **# of Lifetime Page "Likes"** - total number of people who have "Liked" your Page

- **# of Active Users** - how many people have interacted with or viewed your page or posts, including Fans and Non-Fans

Click on "**Insights**" to see the New Likes, Lifetime Likes and Monthly Active Users.

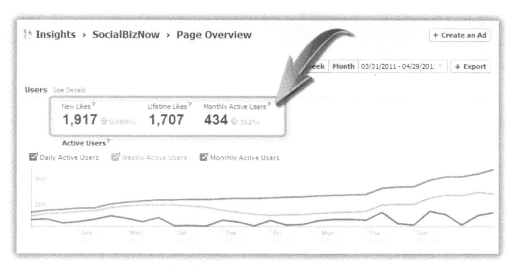

Metrics #2. Page/Custom Tab Views

Tracking the number of visitors to each of your pages and custom tabs is an important metric to determine whether your fans are actually seeing your custom content. You can also compare the number of people visiting your fan page with those who are viewing your custom tab content.

To see statistics by **Page** and **Custom Tab Views,** from the **Page Overview** screen, click the "**See Details**" link next to "**Users**".

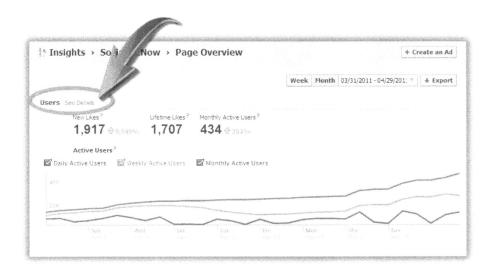

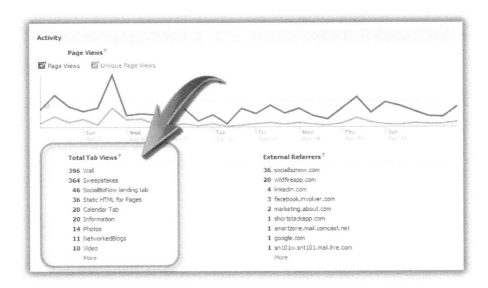

On the **User Detail** page, scroll down to see **Total Tab Views** under the **Activity** section. Click the "**More**" link to see statistics on all tabs.

You can also see where your visitors are coming from in the "**External Referrers**" section.

Metrics #3: Content

Content is measured by the number of views on each post, a metric known as "**Post Impressions**". You can see Content metrics in the "**Interactions**" section of the main Page Overview under Insights.

You can also see the number of Impressions on a specific post and the post Feedback if you're a Page Administrator on the Wall itself, underneath each post.

Metrics #4: Engagement

Engagement includes a number of metrics that are new for most marketers.

These include:

- o **# of Post Views** - the number of times stories on your News feed have been viewed by Fans and Non-Fans

- o **# of Post Feedback** - the number of likes and comments posted on your Page by Fans and Non-Fans

- o **# of Likes on News Feed stories**

- o **# of Comments** - average # of comments per post and total # of comments for the Page

Click the "**See Details**" link next to **Interactions** for detail on engagement metrics, including Feedback, Mentions and Comments by post.

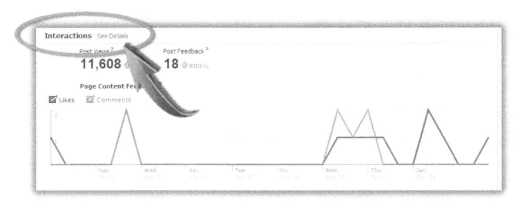

Measuring the Success of Your Page

By understanding the metrics of your Facebook Page, you'll be able to analyze and adjust your marketing efforts. Keep in mind that your goal of measuring the success of your Page is part of your larger online marketing strategy to help your business grow and succeed in some or all of these areas:

- Increase the size of your potential customer pool
- Attract more visitors to your website
- Improve your customers' experience
- Focus your targeting efforts
- Attract more qualified leads
- Generate more inquiries
- Add more opt-ins to mailing list
- Increase the number of conversions
- Increase/Decrease customer touchpoints
- Increase the number of purchases/sales
- Lower the cost to acquire a customer
- Increase revenue
- Improve customer retention
- Increase the number of repeat sales
- Increase cross-sale or up-sell opportunities

A Real-World Guide to Social Media

 Use the <u>**Facebook Marketing Investment Worksheet**</u> at the end of this Chapter to calculate the investment in your Facebook business Page.

Metrics Glossary

Sales Funnel

The series of steps that move a visitor towards a specified conversion event, such as an order or registration signup.

Page View

A request to load a single page of a website. On the web, a page request would result from a web surfer clicking on a link on another page that points to the page in question. Not the same as a "Hit".

Hit

Any request from a file or a web-server. A single page likely contains *multiple* hits as multiple image and text files are downloaded from the web-server.

Unique Visitor

Unique Visitor refers to a single website visitor who interacts with a website over time. The period of time is defined differently from site to site, some sites define the period as 30 minutes or less, others an hour or longer. Therefore the measure of a unique visitor and their activity on a website may be different from one site to another.

Referrer

The location that visitors come from including other websites, search engines or online directories, usually specified as a page location or URL
e.g. *http://www.othersite.com/thatpage.htm*

Search Terms

The terms entered by a visitor that yields a page of search results that may lead a visitor to your website.

Clicks

When someone clicks on a link or image advertisement and lands on another page, this is counted as a Click or "Clickthru".

Exit page

The last page viewed by a visitor on a visitor's path through a site.

Bounce rate

The percentage of entrances on a web page that result in an immediate exit from the web site. For example, if the bounce rate is 44.0% percent on a page, then the number of *direct exits from that page and off that website* is 44 out of 100 visits to that page. If the bounce rate is high (a bounce rate is considered reasonable if it's between 30-40%), then it may indicate a low quality of the content on that page, and the content may need to re-examined or re-written.

Revenue Impact

A measurable correlation between a user's activity on a website and revenue increase or decrease.

Conversion Rate

An action that signifies a completion of a specified activity. For many sites, a user converts if they buy a product, sing up for a newsletter, or download a file. The conversion rate is the percentage of visitors who do convert. Cookie deletion can have an impact on your conversion rate because if a cookie is being systematically deleted, repeat visitor rates will be under-counted and new visitor rates will be over-counted, thus skewing the conversion rate metric by which you analyze your site's overall effectiveness.

Audience Growth

an individual that visits a website. A visitor or unique visitor can have multiple visits and the increase of the number of visits

Facebook Page Marketing Investment Worksheet

Business Name:		
Prepared by:		
Date:		

Task Description	Investment	
	Time	**Financial**
	# of hrs (total or per day/wk/month)	$$$ e.g. Equipment, Vendors
Page Setup		
Page Maintenance		
Content Posting		
Analysis		
Research		
(add your own tasks here)		

Summary

Facebook has evolved into a powerhouse for businesses, for connecting and sharing with customers, for finding and targeting new markets, for gaining competitive share and driving sales.

By beginning your journey into the world of Social Media and Facebook with this eBook, you've taken a step forward into the new world of online marketing, digital media and advertising.

Next steps on your journey are continuing to actively promote your business Page, analyzing your efforts, measuring results, and making sure you monitor your brand while managing your risks.

It's a lot to take in, but then again, this is a whole new world of how we connect with our customers - and a whole new way of doing business.

Facebook by the #s

1	Facebook users can only have one username for their personal profile.
1	Facebook Page administrators can only have one username for each Page
1	You may only create one Facebook Advertising account per currency.
5	The minimum number of characters in a Username.
20	The maximum number of Facebook friends or email addresses you can message at one time.
25	The minimum number of "likes" required before you can register a username for a business Page.
25	The minimum number of "likes" required before you can edit a business Page username.
25	You can target each Facebook Ad to up to 25 countries.
30	The minimum number of users required to "Like" a business Page before Insights (Facebook's built-in metrics) will start showing up for the page.
100	The maximum number of photos you can upload into a Mobile Uploads album, before a second album is automatically created.
100	The maximum number of "likes" on a business Page after which you cannot edit the business Name.
100	The maximum number of people you can invite to an event at a time.

100	The maximum number of friend lists you can have.
200	The maximum number of photos you can upload per album.
250	Admins of groups with fewer than 250 people can change the privacy setting of their groups.
300	The maximum number of groups you can join.
300	The maximum number of pending invites at one time for an event
500	The maximum number of Pages you can "like".
1000	The maximum number of friends you can have per friend list. You can have the same friend on multiple lists.
5000	The maximum number of friends you can have on a personal Profile.
Unlimited	There is no limit to the number of Pages you can manage -you can manage as many Pages as you have been given the authority to manage.
Unlimited	You can invite an unlimited number of people to events
Unlimited	You can have as many applications as you want on Facebook.
Unlimited	You can have unlimited photo albums on Facebook.
Unlimited	A business Page can have unlimited "likes".

About the Author

Roohi Moolla
CEO/Founder
SocialBiz*Now* | Neighborhood*Now*

www.socialbiznow.com | www.neighborhoodnow.com
roohi@socialbiznow.com
Twitter: @roohimoolla
Facebook: www.facebook.com/roohimoolla
LinkedIn: www.linkedin.com/in/roohimoolla

Roohi Moolla has over 28 years of experience spanning careers in Architecture and Information Technology. As an Architect, Ms. Moolla was involved in the design and development of a number of large-scale residential and commercial ventures in Toronto, Canada.

Over the past 16 years, Roohi has successfully designed, developed and implemented numerous commercial website and e-commerce solutions for a variety of industries including telecommunications, social networking, construction, and finance as well as websites for organizations in the private and public sector. Ms. Moolla has been involved with a number of software startups, including the dating site that became Match.com, a proprietary Bid/RFP procurement and subscription system (now publicly traded as Onvia) and a Syndicate Municipal Bond Trading platform, BondDesk Syndicate.

Ms. Moolla is the Founder and CEO of Neighborhoodnow.com, a network of online social calendar and community portals connecting people and communities through events and news, and CEO and Founder of SocialBizNow, a new media and technology blog that provides information to businesses on Social Media tools, techniques, strategies and best practices. She is also an active speaker and author on topics related to Social Media and Technology, and is the Producer of SocialBizWorld, a Social Media Conference held north of San Francisco.

Ms. Moolla holds a Bachelor of Environmental Studies from the University of Manitoba and a Bachelor of Architecture from the University of Arizona, and is a Microsoft Certified Professional.

INDEX